Literacy Begins at Birth

Literacy Begins at Birth

A revolutionary approach in whole language learning. Emphasizes writing before reading in early childhood.

Dr. Marjorie V. Fields, Ed.D.

FISHER BOOKS

Publishers	Bill Fisher
and	Helen Fisher
Editors:	Howard Fisher
	Tom Monroe, P.E.
Art Director:	Josh Young

Published by Fisher Books
P.O. Box 38040
Tucson, Arizona 85740-8040

(602) 325-5263

Library of Congress Cataloging-in-Publication Data
Fields, Marjorie Vannoy.
    Literacy begins at birth.

    Includes index.
    1. Reading (Preschool & Primary School)—United States—Language experience approach. 2. Language arts (Preschool)—United States. I. Title.
LB1181.33.F54 1988 649'.58 88-24620
ISBN 1-55561-014-5

©1989 Fisher Books

Printed in U.S.A.
Printing 10 9 8 7 6 5 4 3 2

Notice: The information in this book is true and complete to the best of our knowledge. It is offered with no guarantees on the part of the author or Fisher Books. The author and publisher disclaim all liability in connection with the use of this book.

Fisher Books are available at special quantity discounts for educational use. Special books, or book excerpts, can also be created to fit specific needs. For details please write or telephone.

Contents

Guidelines for Using this Book ix

Section 1: How Children Learn to Read & Write . . . 1

1. Reading All Around Us 3
2. Mystery Messages: Children's Early Writing 11
3. Listening & Talking, Reading & Writing . .23
4. Playing Around & Getting Around 35

Section 2: Your Infant Starts on Road to Literacy . .47

5. Defeating Boredom; Enemy of Learning . .49
6. A Language-rich Environment 61

Section 3: Your Toddler Becomes Aware of
Reading & Writing 71

7. First Words 73
8. Learning & Doing 83
9. Wonderful Scribbles 97
10. Please Don't Eat the Books 103

Section 4: Your Preschooler Gains
Understanding of Print 113

11. An Explosion of Language 115
12. Read it Again 127
13. I Sure Said Lots of Words 139
14. What Does It Say? 151
15. Let's Pretend 161
16. I Go to School 177

Section 5: Your Primary-grader Begins to
Read & Write 193

17. A Writer in a Literate Society 195
18. You Read & Then I Read 213
19. Learning by Doing 225
20. Choosing the Very Best 239
21. Trouble-shooting 251

Accomplished, Eager Readers & Writers 267
Bibliography 269
Index 271

For my wonderful sons, Michael and David.
You give meaning to my life.

Acknowledgments

Because this book is about real people, I have imposed on many wonderful people in order to write it. I am impressed with the generosity of parents in sharing their experiences for the benefit of other parents. The delightful children who allowed me into their lives to do my research have been a source of inspiration to me. It seems that these children and their parents actually wrote this book: Patrick McCormick, Christy Keller, Jordan Kendall, Brianna Ackley, Alex Creekman, Corey Denton, Tanya Roust, Summer and Roz Koester and Ashley Capps. The children and teachers at the University of Alaska Southeast Child Care Center also played a significant role, as did Vivian Montoya and her kindergarten class.

The people who gave their time to critique sections of this book as it was written also made a major contribution to its completion. I wish to thank Joanne Zenter, Margo Waring, Valerie Truce, Vivian Montoya, Reggie Johnson and my husband, Don. Don and my sons, Michael and David, are to be thanked for their patience and support while I wrote and worked under deadlines.

Author and kids in the book: In back, son David, author and Tanya; in front, Corey, Christy and Patrick.

About the Author

Dr. Marjorie Vannoy Fields, parent, author and teacher, is a Professor of Early Childhood Education at the University of Alaska Southwest at Juneau. Her teaching career began as a kindergarten teacher and she later taught first grade. In 1978, she received her doctorate in early-childhood education.

As a former member of the Governing Board of the National Association for the Education of Young Children, her scope of concerns encompassed all issues impacting the quality of life for young children. Board responsibilities included working with early-child educators around the country to develop education guidelines for young children and to establish standards for accreditation of preschools.

Marjorie's national reputation is reflected in her election as a Board member of the National Association for Early Childhood Teacher Educators. Additionally, she serves on the Teacher Education Advisory Panel, which reviews Early Childhood Education programs for national accreditation.

Marjorie authored *Let's Begin Reading Right: a developmental approach to beginning literacy*, a textbook for teachers widely used in colleges and universities in the United States. She has also written articles on early-childhood education, some of which have appeared in *Principal,* the journal of the National Association of Elementary School Principals, and the *Reading Teacher,* journal of the International Readers Association. These writings and frequent presentations at professional meetings have required Marjorie to stay current with the latest research on beginning literacy by colleagues around the world.

As a parent and teacher, Dr. Fields utilized her own advice in raising her two sons. This experience as a parent gives Marjorie additional insights about how children learn and about the parenting process.

Guidelines for Using This Book

This book is set up to make it easy for you as a parent to find specific information you need, when you need it. For example, if you are currently focused on your preschool child's needs, you shouldn't have to wade through information about infants or first graders. That is why the book is divided into sections according to stages of early childhood.

In addition to reading the section about kids the same age as yours, read Section 1, How Children Learn to Read & Write. This section explains general principles that apply to all early age groups. These explanations should help you understand more fully those given in other sections of the book.

Section 1 also explains the Whole Language teaching process that is sweeping the United States. It demonstrates how oral and written language interrelate by comparing a child's progress in learning to talk with progress in learning how to write. Section 1 also discusses other Whole Language principles. It gives examples of how children learn to read and write from experiencing our print-rich environment and being a part of our literate society. This foundation section includes guidelines for assisting your child's general-knowledge base and intellectual development. These are important components of a successful introduction to reading and writing.

Each subsequent section provides information

and suggestions specific to early age groups. Each discusses age-appropriate reading, writing, books and experiences. As an example, the infant section discusses reading to your baby as part of language development, but recommends that you start this important activity in infancy. You may be surprised to find a chapter on writing in the toddler section. Experiences are emphasized in every section, both for intellectual development and for language development.

Most people readily accept that reading and writing are related. And most have little difficulty with the idea that oral- and written-language learning are similar. The suggestion that children need real-life experiences before they read makes sense to most people, too. Most also accept that children need experiences in order to have something to talk and write about. But when we tell them that children need to play as part of reading and writing, some people start to have doubts.

Play as exploration of the environment, discovering knowledge and learning to think is explained for each age level. This helps parents understand more about the *intellectual* base for their child's literacy. Play as a builder of self-confidence and personal autonomy is also explained for each age. This helps parents understand more about the *emotional* base for their child's literacy.

Literacy Begins at Birth focuses on the whole child as it discusses how children learn to read and write. These literacy skills do not happen in a vacuum. A child may be rendered incapable of learning by teaching approaches that push on one area at the expense of another.

Parents share the education of their children with teachers and caregivers. This is acknowledged in chapters giving guidelines for selecting the best schools and childcare situations for nurturing your child's emerging literacy. The fact that sometimes things go awry at school is acknowledged in Chapter 21, Trouble-shooting.

This book offers you a friendly hand as you meet the daily challenges of guiding your child's growth. Experiences and advice of other parents meeting those same challenges are here for you. Research and advice of experts studying how children learn are here for you, too. May they make your role as a parent easier and the results more satisfying.

Section 1

How Children Learn to Read & Write

Children see reading and writing all around them. Their print-rich environment makes them want to read, too.

1

Reading All Around Us

Children learn to read and write in much the same way they learn to listen and speak. Being around people who talk makes the baby want to talk and also provides essential instruction for learning how to talk. Similarly, being around people who read and write makes children eager to learn reading and writing. It also gives them major insights about the process. This idea is significant in light of new understandings of how children become literate, called the *Whole Language philosophy*. Examples and suggestions in this book for helping your child master written language are derived from new research demonstrating the validity of a Whole Language approach.

This approach utilizes real-life reading experiences to introduce youngsters to what reading is all about. The signs, books, newspapers, labels and grocery lists that are a part of our everyday lives constitute what is called the *print-rich environment*. These are a part of the world your child is so eagerly exploring and are important tools for beginning reading and writing. Children are keen

Patrick sees grownups reading the newspaper, so he is very interested in it, too. When you sit down with your newspaper, you are helping your child learn to read.

observers and learn about many uses of print at an early age simply by being exposed to written language. They notice whether books are considered important and entertaining to the adults around them. They notice that big people write down important things they want to remember. They also notice what the sign looks like for *Coke* and other things we wish they wouldn't recognize.

Taking time to read to your children almost assures that they will love to read.

Parents who are readers

Did you realize that when you sit down with the newspaper, you are helping your child learn to read? If you have the energy and can force yourself to let your youngster look on with you for a few minutes and discuss some of the headlines or pictures, then you are helping even more. But just seeing *you* reading is the main thing. This is how children find out that reading is worth their while. This is how they become curious about reading and start trying to figure it out.

Without this basic introduction to reading, any other instruction is without foundation. The more your child is aware of the importance of reading in *your* life, the firmer the foundation for learning to read. When children hear their parents discuss books that are entertaining or articles that offer useful information, this too builds that foundation. Children's natural desire to do the things they see grown-ups doing makes reading seem to run in families. Children of eager readers are usually eager readers themselves.

Taking time to read to your children almost assures they will love to read. Research shows that being read to is the one common factor in the backgrounds of successful readers. When you share books with children, not only do they see you reading, they also are looking at and trying to make sense of the page you are reading from. Depending upon the child's level, this may be examining the pictures for detail, trying to figure out which letters say which word, or even grabbing a page to taste it—a common response to quality literature.

In addition to intellectual gains, the emotional aspect of storytime with a parent has a significant impact on future reading. The loving closeness of these special times together creates good feelings that carry over to good feelings about books and reading. Reading to your child is an important part of creating a life-long love of reading.

Parents who are writers

Does your child see you write? You may not have thought about this before. Seeing their parents writing makes children want to write. And it teaches them a great deal about how and why people write. When we watch youngsters explore with pen and paper, we can observe what they are learning about how to hold a pen or pencil. We can also tell what they are learning about how writing looks. If we listen to what they tell us about their writing or if we overhear them talking to themselves as they write, we can find out a lot about what they think writing is for. Many children know about making lists for shopping. Most know about writing down phone messages. Some know about writing letters and a few even know about expressing themselves through poetry. When children realize that what is written down can be read by others, they begin to have a better understanding of what reading is.

When a child also realizes that what he *says* can be written down and read by others, he achieves a major breakthrough. Writing children's thoughts and ideas for them as they dictate to you is a wonderfully effective way to teach reading. Watching a little face light up as someone reads that child's words can show us how important this experience is to the youngster. It is essential that you write exactly what your child says—poor grammar, incomplete sentences and all. If you try to *clean it up* by correcting these deficiencies as you write, then the words read back are not the child's. The

Writing children's thoughts and ideas for them as they dictate to you is an effective way to teach reading.

excitement of recognizing his or her own words will be missing and the realization that *reading is talk written down* will be lost.

When you write for a child, try to sit so the youngster can see what you're doing. If you are right-handed, it is best if the child is on your left so your hand isn't in the way. This way children who are ready to notice can watch and learn about how to hold a pencil, how letters are formed, what side of the page to start writing on, and other writing mechanics such as spaces between words and punctuation. This is called *The Language Experience Approach to Reading* and is an important part of most beginning reading programs.

Sometimes writing for children happens informally as part of play, such as when Brandon wants a sign on his block tower that says, "Do not wreck." Summer sometimes asks for help in writing on *tickets* to the plays she and her sister perform for their parents. Summer wants help writing a menu for playing restaurant on occasion, but she also may decide to write for herself and spell words the way they sound to her. Either approach—or a combination—teaches her about reading and writing.

Reading skills

Children can read these words they dictate or request because they have personal meaning. A child who is excited about *dinosaurs* may read that word before much shorter ones. Another child may begin by reading the word *astronaut*. OK, maybe it is more remembering than reading at first; but kids who can link written words (print) with the ideas they represent are making progress in reading. These first *remembered* words become their initial sight-word vocabulary and provide a basis for learning other words. Phonics concepts make some sense when they are based on what children already know. Children learn phonics and other reading skills best when they are encouraged to discover the concepts through their own experiences with print. When Brianna suddenly realizes that two of her favorite words, *Daddy* and *dinosaur,* start with the same letter **D** and the same sound, she makes a major breakthrough in her understanding of written language. We need to be sure children have the *big picture* of what reading is before we start on the details. This means making sure children understand *what reading is* and *what it is for* before we try to teach them about specific letters and sounds.

Children see writing and reading used for a variety of purposes and want to explore those uses. They ask endless questions about "what does that say?" They learn to recognize and read print on cereal boxes, in their favorite books, on the advertising billboard and on the corner stop sign. At first they can only recognize the word *STOP* when it is on a red octagonal sign at the intersection; but eventually they will recognize that word elsewhere. All these experiences of being immersed in the print-rich environment of this literate society will one day result in your child bringing you a book and saying with surprised delight, "I can read this!"

Some Ways Children Learn to Read:
* Seeing others read
* Being read to
* Seeing others write
* Having someone write for them
* Figuring out print for themselves

2

Mystery Messages: Children's Early Writing

Stages of writing development are a fascinating part of your child's growth as a reader and writer. Did you know that even random scribbles on a page (or wall) are the beginnings of writing?

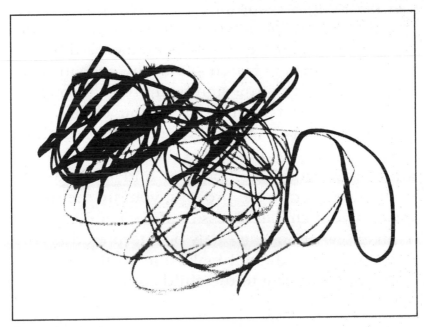

Scribble stage

Scribble stage

Scribbling is the stage of exploring to find out what happens when a crayon or pencil moves on a surface. We adults may have trouble seeing the value in this very basic experimentation. However, if we understand what is happening, we can provide the materials and encouragement to assist in the learning process.

Scribbling is an important first stage of writing. Your child must go through it to get to the next. Writing is an important part of learning about reading; reading and writing go hand-in-hand, just like talking and understanding the speech of others.

Linear, repetitive stage

Before long, your little scribbler begins to notice that big people's writing looks different from his or hers. Then the scribbles take on a different look: they begin to march across the page in semi-straight lines. This is a significant breakthrough—one that is best learned from the child's own observations. If you try to explain this sort of thing before your child has noticed it, you are talking about something unimportant and irrelevant to your youngster. In the process, you run the risk of making your child feel less confident and capable. Your explanations can easily be interpreted as criticism and certainly will make the writing process seem more baffling to the child.

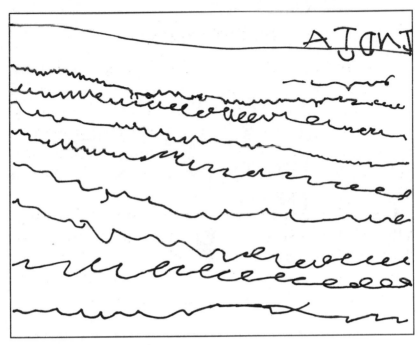

Linear, repetitive stage

About the same time scribbles start being put in lines, you will notice that they have also become quite repetitious. Some children tend to make rows and rows of small circle shapes, others make rows of loops or waves. Whatever the form, we can see that writing appears to the child as an incomprehensible series of marks that all look pretty much alike. Differences in types of marks suggest that youngsters sometimes are trying to print and sometimes trying to write in longhand like grownups. Observing as your child gradually figures out more and more of the characteristics of writing gives you a window into his mind. You will be able to see each exciting new discovery demonstrated as your child's understanding about writing evolves.

Combination of letter and letter-like forms and other symbols.

Letter-like stage

The marks your child makes to represent writing will gradually start to look like letters. I didn't say they *were* letters, notice. I said they *look* like letters. Youngsters notice the general look of letters before they have an understanding of specific letters. They notice that letters tend to be made up of lines and circles in various combinations. So you might see something like a **T**, but with extra crosses; or something like a **B**, but with three seg-

14

ments instead of two. We needn't worry about children making their letters incorrectly. This is just another stage of learning about writing. In fact, attempts to correct these strangely creative letter-like forms can cause your child to stop trying to write independently. This can start a pattern of looking to adults for answers rather than thinking and trying to figure out things alone.

The learning process

I worry quite a bit about youngsters who have had well-meaning adults making an issue of forming letters exactly right. I also worry about youngsters who were given lessons in the sounds of letters before they could generate their own hypotheses about letters and sounds. Unless a child is very self-confident, this will stop the free exploration that results in discovery learning.

Learning through exploration and discovery results in true learning and understanding, as opposed to superficial *rote learning*—by memory alone, without understanding or thought.

If we want children to understand a concept, we must help them discover it for themselves and make it their own. Too often we simply tell children how things are supposed to be in an attempt to impose our adult understandings upon them. If we want children to have confidence in themselves as learners and to be excited about trying to learn new things, we must accept their level of knowing and their ways of learning.

Beginning invented spelling

Invented spelling

Your acceptance continues to be necessary as your child begins to try out some more hypotheses about the nature of writing. When beginners tackle spelling, they do it their way. They figure out ways of spelling that make sense to them. Researchers call this the *Invented Spelling Stage.*

As children discover specific letters, they begin to notice relationships between the letters and the sounds of words. At first they only notice the first sound in a word, then usually will add the last sound, and sometime later attempt the in-between

Beginners figure out ways of spelling that make sense to *them.*This is called *Invented Spelling.*

sounds. So for awhile, you may see single letters used to represent whole words.

Generally children's beginning phonics hypothesis is that letters make the sounds of their own name: This works for many letters most of the time, such as b, d, f, j, k, l, m, n, p, r, s, t, v and z. However, it results in interesting spellings such as the letter **Y** for the word *once* and the letter **H** for words beginning with *CH*. If you don't understand why children choose these substitutions, say the letter names to yourself and hear the sounds.

As youngsters begin to notice that most words have several letters in them, they tend to place

Manuel is starting to notice that books have words as well as pictures. This new observation is related to his experiments with writing. Children's powers of observation become keener once they are writers. They are now ready to see subtle things about words that previously escaped them.

random letters to fill out the amount of space they estimate is appropriate for a given word. Because they initially consider the written word to be a picture of the *thing* it stands for, children commonly believe that the word for something big must be a big word and the word for something small must be a small word. Similarly, they believe Daddy's name must be longer than their own.

Standardized spelling begins

Their powers of observation become keener once they themselves are writers. They notice the writing of others in books, newspapers, signs and

the tigr and me   i had a pat tigr
he aet the carrots aoot of my mommy.s
grden my mommy ded not cer ef he ded
win nit i hrd a ciode haooling any my
tigr hesing at the ciote i got up to
sees wut wis gowing on aoot sid so i
die   i so my tigr he had a brocen lag
i asct my mommy to breing my tige to
the vet and so she ded   the end

Advanced invented spelling

grocery lists. They are now ready to see subtle things about words that escaped them previously. They are strongly motivated to make their writing as *grown-up* as possible. They can read their own writing and this helps them learn to read the writing of others. They start to notice when their formation of a word is different from someone else's. Gradually, you will see your child's writing begin to conform to standard spelling.

It may seem at times that spelling gets worse at this point. You may be worried because your child starts to put a silent **e** on the end of every word, or begins inserting a silent **gh** in strange places. Don't worry, this just shows a new awareness of phonics principles and experimentation with them. This overuse of certain spellings will soon disappear, with continued awareness of standard spelling forms.

You will probably continue to see these types of errors as your child's knowledge of writing continues to expand. You may see some strange ways of separating words. For instance, some children decide to put periods or lines between words for awhile to make sure they are separated. As periods and other forms of punctuation are discovered, you will see them used in novel ways at first.

If you are like me, you will be sorry when your youngster progresses beyond these personal interpretations and writes like everyone else. Of course you are pleased with the progress, but you have lost that window into the thinking process. It makes me think of how I felt when my oldest child learned to walk. Of course I wanted him to walk, but it was absolute evidence that he was no longer a baby. There is a touch of nostalgia in these advances.

Overcoming improper teaching

Your pleasure in your child's writing experiments and your encouragement to continue trying is especially necessary if your child has been *taught* about writing by copying correctly spelled words. This was a common teaching practice prior to recent research findings about how children really learn to read and write. We used to think that children had to first learn all the letter shapes and their sounds. Then they could learn to put those sounds together to figure out words and would be able to read. And, finally, they could memorize how writing looked and be able to use writing as a tool.

In the past few years professionals studying beginning literacy around the world have discovered that this sequence is backwards from how children really learn. This old approach can get in the way of children's real learning. It is likely to teach children merely to accept what they are told instead of teaching them to think and strive for understanding. It can keep them from becoming confident, from enjoying the process and, therefore, from achieving real proficiency as writers.

Stages of Writing Development:
* Scribbling
* Linear-Repetitive
* Letter-like Forms
* Invented Spelling
* Standard Spelling

3

Listening & Talking,
Reading & Writing

Newborn babies make a lot of sounds—some we like; some we don't like. These sounds are the beginnings of speech, though they don't bear much resemblance to it for awhile. From the start, the ability to make sounds helps the baby to get vital needs met. Babies quickly learn that their voices can bring someone with food or a dry diaper.

In the process of getting some nice warm milk or a lovely dry diaper, babies tend to see and hear people making a variety of sounds. These people smile and make even more sounds when the baby makes sounds. How interesting this game must seem. Have you ever seen a very young baby watching you talk and moving his or her little tongue and lips around as if in imitation? Your child wants to do the things you do. Language, whether spoken or written, is an important part of the world and youngsters want to participate in it. Because spoken language is the basis of written language,

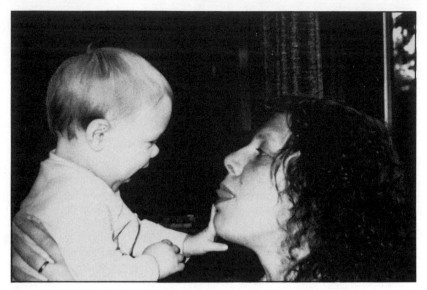

Patrick is fascinated by the sounds of language.

a good vocabulary and fluency with speech is the beginning of learning to read and write.

We see that the process for learning to talk is much like the process for learning to read and write. Examining how children become fluent with oral language can help us to understand much about how they become fluent with written language.

Speaking and writing are the *output* forms of language; hearing and reading are the *input* forms. It is difficult to study how children gain competence with input, but we can easily study their output. We can compare their beginning speech with their beginning writing. I find this a fascinating study.

Messing around with language

At first babies just randomly explore what their voices will do. First babblings and cooings have no relationship to any language. In fact, young babies are versatile linguists with the ability to make the sounds of all the world's languages. Little French babies may accidentally make the gutteral sounds of German so foreign to their native language and little Japanese babies may make those English **L** and **R** sounds that are so difficult for their parents.

This random exploration of sounds is much like the scribble stage of writing. In both cases, the youngster is just *messing around with the materials*—whether it be making random sounds or random marks on paper. Both babbling and scribbling are important first explorations of a language medium. Both show children's interest in the language around them and their eagerness to participate in it. Both need and deserve your encouragement.

What did she say?

Do you remember when the sounds your baby made started to sound like real talking? Sometime in the second half of the first year, most babies start to string sounds together with the intonations of the language around them. You probably did the same thing I did—tried to figure out what your youngster was saying. Only after careful listening over a period of time did I come to the conclusion that there were no words in all those language sounds. Wade's mother tells about listening to him talk on a phone with no one on the line. He jabbers away animatedly for awhile, occasionally punctuating his gibberish with laughs; then he stops and sits in silence a bit as if listening before he continues to make talking sounds. It's pretty clear that Wade is a good observer of telephone talking behavior, even if he can't talk yet. Similarly, children observe and learn much about the nature of writing before they are ready to write actual letters or words. They show us this when they write those lines of squiggles across a page in their linear-repetitive stage of writing.

He said, "Mama!"

Were you thrilled when your youngster first said "ma" or "da?" These aren't real words, but they are close enough that we accept them as having meaning. These and other word-like sounds, such as "ba" for *ball* or *bottle,* represent another breakthrough in a child's understanding of language and ability to control it.

Children at this stage have identified and mastered some of the general language patterns around them; they now focus on specific sounds of their native language. The excited response they get from their parents encourages babies to continue making those sounds. Can you see the similarity between this word-like stage of oral language and the letter-like stage of written language described in the last chapter? In each case, children have noticed detail and figured out what details are significant. They no longer merely make strings of

Alex's vocabulary is growing by leaps and bounds. There are many exciting things to talk about. Spoken language is the basis of written language. A good vocabulary and fluency with speech is the beginning of learning to read and write.

A chat with an adult who listens carefully and respectfully is an important part of language development. Talking with and listening to him or her helps your child become proficient with language.

sounds or strings of marks; they now are striving for the precision of specific sounds and specific marks.

Baby talk

A child's tentative word-like sounds gradually evolve into real words. These first words are not perfectly articulated, nor are they part of complete sentences. However, they communicate effectively to the tuned-in ear. If you spend much time around a young child, you learn the unique characteristics of *baby talk* and can decipher the message. Each child's early speech seems to have its own idiosyncrasies, such as my son Mike's word "gung" for *lift me up* or *I want that up there.* Yet, there are common principles that describe baby-talk in general.

Keeping it simple

Simplification is the rule governing beginning speech. Simplification can be accomplished by omitting the ending sound or syllable of a word: For 2-year-old Davey "no" means *nose* and "tee" means *teeth,* while "bot" serves for *bottle.* Sometimes Davey leaves off the beginning sound instead and says "ummy" for *tummy* or "urt" for *hurt.* Another simplification strategy, which you will recognize if you are familiar with young children's speech, is to use the same sounds or same types of sounds at the beginning and end of a word. This explains why "guck" commonly represents *truck* to a toddler. The **g** sound is a version of the **k** sound. If you don't believe that, say each sound to yourself and you will feel that each is made in the same part of your throat, one with vocal chords and one only with forced air.

A similar principle is shown when a youngster simplifies two-syllable words by making both syllables identical: Davey calls himself "Deedee" and adults acknowledge this tendency when they call themselves "mama" or "dada." Early sentence construction also follows the simplification rule. Toddlers speak in *telegraph sentences* such as "Me go" or "aw (all) gone" and communicate a variety of meanings without the complication of adjectives, adverbs or other modifiers.

Beginning invented-spelling principles have much in common with beginning-speech principles. When a child writes a word with just one letter, that is simplification, which makes the task of writing manageable for a beginner. The assumption that our sound-symbol system is a logical one, where all letters make the sound of their name, is another excellent simplification strategy. While this works for most letters, it creates confusion for adults not used to seeing the word *once* spelled with a **Y**.

Creative grammar

As children progress toward speaking in sentences, they try to make sense of the *rules* of language—what we call *grammar*. They are pretty clear about the subject-verb-object sequence: A child never says, "candy eat me." If we turn the usual pattern around and say something like "Mommy was kissed by Davey," the child will understand it as "Mommy kissed Davey." Children try to find consistent patterns upon which to formulate their own grammar rules. Even though they do this unconsciously, we can hear what they are doing. When they say, "I wented to the store," we can be sure they didn't hear that from us. This is an example of overgeneralizing the common rule that we add *ed* for the past tense. Of course a young child could never explain this rule, but we can hear it in operation. The rule for forming plurals is also overgeneralized, so youngsters often say they have "two foots."

Few adults worry about these grammatical errors or make a point of correcting them. We accept them as part of the charm of young children's language with the calm assurance that they will soon disappear. We simply say, "Yes, you have two cute little feet." Yet adults tend to get concerned about similar overgeneralization errors in children's beginning spelling. They become afraid that the child who spells "permission" as "permishen" will never spell correctly. So, instead of enjoying what the child wrote and being thrilled that the child is writing, adults point out the errors. If we did this for beginning speech, we would find children reluctant to talk. It is no fun to try when you know you are going to be criticized for your efforts. Is it any wonder that teachers with red pencils make students reluctant to write?

Confidence instead of criticism

Whether a child is learning to talk or to write, continued exposure to correct forms will cause self-correction of most errors. To assist your child's proficiency with oral language, you primarily need to talk and listen to him or her. Similarly, to assist your child's proficiency with written language, you primarily need to read with him or her and encourage independent writing. Confidence in your child's ability to learn to talk helps you to respond uncritically to beginning speech. The same confidence in your child's ability and drive to crack the code of written language can guide you in a similar uncritical response to beginning writing. With an understanding of how the two learning processes are similar, parents can teach their children to read as successfully as they teach them to talk.

It has been said:

**If we taught children to talk
like we teach them to read,
We would have a lot of non-talkers.**

Let us say instead:

**If we taught children to read
the way we teach them to talk,
We would have few non-readers.**

LANGUAGE DEVELOPMENT		
ORAL LANGUAGE	WRITTEN LANGUAGE	UNDERSTANDING LEVEL
Babbling and Cooing	Scribbling Stage	Exploration of Medium
Language Intonation	Linear/Repetitive Stage	Refining the Form
Native Language Sounds	Letter-like Forms	Cultural Relevance
Words	Letters and Early Word Symbol Relationships	Conventions of Language
Creative Grammar	Invented Spelling	Overgeneralization of "Rule" Hypotheses
"Adult Speech"	Standard Spelling	Formal Structure

Similar stages of talking and writing do not occur at the same ages, but they do occur in the same sequence.

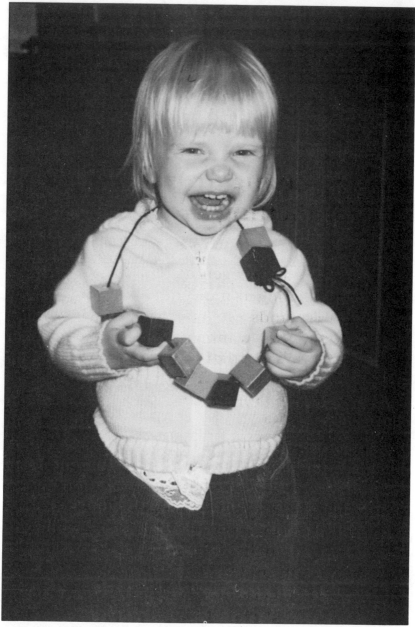

Children are always getting into things. How wonderful that they are so driven to learn and grow.

4

Playing Around & Getting Around

Children are always getting into things. They insist upon exploring as much of their world as they can get their hands on. They are hungry for experiences; always wanting to touch what they shouldn't, to do what they are too little to do, to go with you when you haven't time for the extra bother. How wonderful that children are so driven to learn and grow!

Because our children demand to explore and experience the world, parents make provisions for these needs. We also meet these needs just because we love to see the joy and excitement that new experiences can bring to our children's faces. Phoebe enjoys Shawn's delight as she helps her toddler gently pet a kitty and feel its soft fur. Jim lets Brandon "help" him take a load of things to the dump and sees how grown-up and important his son feels. Mike and Katy began taking Patrick out for walks when he was a week old; he was already bored with hanging around the house.

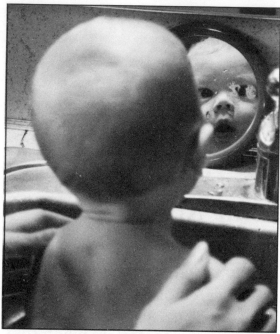

Children need to explore their world by touching, tasting, smelling, hearing and acting upon things.

Learning through experience

Although you provide experiences like these for your child, it's possible you don't fully realize the educational value of those experiences. Research on intellectual development shows that first-hand experiences are essential to a child's learning. Children only truly understand that which they discover as they explore their surroundings. They do not fully grasp those things that an adult merely tells them. In fact, telling kids things may hinder their learning by keeping them from thinking for themselves.

Thinking is the key to real learning. Trying to

figure things out is much more valuable than trying to remember what someone told you. Even though the answer you get for yourself may be wrong at first, you have accomplished more than by memorizing someone else's right answer. When children come up with their own explanations, they are beginning a process of life-long inquiry into the nature of objects, events and people. We adults cannot possibly know what questions and issues these youngsters may face 30 or 40 years from now. The best preparation we can give them is confidence in themselves as thinkers, plus practice in seeking answers. Merely giving them answers is short-sighted.

Accepting mistakes allows learning

When Shawn points to a picture of a beaver and says, "kitty!" Phoebe doesn't worry about correcting him. He is using his past experience to make sense of a new one, so his interpretation shows thought and learning. Phoebe knows his knowledge will increase as his experiences increase. Shawn's *mistake* is not only a result of his limited experiences, but also an example of how children's learning progresses. They understand general concepts before they are able to pick up on the subtleties of detail. For instance, they often know the category *dog* at an early age and proceed to call all four-legged animals *doggy* until they are old enough and experienced enough to see the difference between a dog in the neighborhood and a deer in the woods. Similarly, they know the idea of *going bye-bye* long before they are able to differentiate and respond to going to the store versus going to the park. We know that youngsters must grasp the big picture before they can tune-in to details. This helps us to understand why youngsters must understand what reading and writing are before they can learn about letters or words.

Are you uncomfortable with letting a mistaken idea go uncorrected? Experts who have done extensive research on how children learn assure us that simply correcting children's immature thinking is counterproductive. If you tell Monique that she has just as much juice in her wide, short glass as Nicholas has in his tall, narrow glass, Monique will only become confused. To her, it is clear that the tall glass has more juice; but adults clearly know everything and can't be wrong. She is confused. What Monique learns from being told something beyond her ability to understand is that her own ideas can't be counted on. She learns to mistrust her own thinking and instead to rely on an authority to tell her what to think.

Instead of telling children right answers when theirs are wrong, parents can help by providing experiences that assist children to discover or figure out better answers. I say *better* rather than *right* because it may take quite awhile before a youngster can replace an immature understanding with an adult one. Like the ability to perceive that different-shape glasses can contain the same amount of liquid, much of learning must wait for maturation. Monique will continue to insist on a tall narrow glass for several more years, no matter what experiences she has. She will also continue to prefer three pennies to one nickel and prefer a *big* nickel to a dime. Phoebe knows Monique will figure out which buys more soon enough.

Play and learning

The kinds of experiences that help your child learn best involve manipulation and exploration of real things like sand and water. Children need to explore their world by touching, tasting, smelling, hearing, seeing and acting upon things. Through their senses, children gather data for thoughtful analysis that leads to understanding. Only gradually do they develop the ability to think independently of this type of experience. Play is the perfect way for children to do their exploring. That is what play is all about; the natural way for youngsters to learn what they need and want to learn.

Active not passive

It is important for children to have play materials that encourage thoughtful exploration and action in general. Some toys do all the playing for a child, leaving the youngster merely to sit and watch as a battery-powered toy does things. Some toys do so much for children that no thought or problem-solving is needed. How sad that in many homes readymade sophisticated play tents have replaced the challenge of making a cozy tent under a table covered with blankets that have to be anchored on. By contrast, blocks invite children to become actively involved. When youngsters play with blocks, they must think for themselves about what to do and then how to do it. Art media such as finger paints or play dough present the same opportunity. These are materials that can be used in a variety of ways involving open-ended creative self-expression, problem-solving and thinking in general.

Real not plastic

Some parents are aware that young children need real things to manipulate for play, but don't realize that a toy plastic cow is a symbol of something real rather than being real itself. The plastic cow is real in that it can be touched and moved, but it is only a real piece of plastic.

The replica of a cow has meaning and can be effective in a child's thoughtful play after that child has experienced an actual cow. With real experience as the base, the toy cow becomes a meaningful symbol for something real to the child. With actual experience, the child also has understanding to bring to other symbols such as pictures and stories about cows. Often children will want to symbolize their experience for themselves by pretending to be a cow, drawing pictures of cows or dictating a story about seeing a cow. The first-hand experience is the base upon which the written and spoken word must build.

Maybe you are the kind of parent who lets children play with real things such as pots and pans

Do you let your child help with cooking? Cooking is not only great fun for little kids, it is a superb learning activity.

in the kitchen. Do you also let them help with simple cooking? Mixing, pouring and flipping pancakes for breakfast is not only great fun for little kids, it is a great learning activity. A child can learn about reading a recipe, about measuring and fractions, and about what heat does to liquid. A lot of fine-muscle coordination is involved in all the processes. Have you noticed that helping with work tends to be a favorite form of play for children? Of course this stops when they are actually old enough to be a real help.

Symbolic representation

When they can't help out with real work, children can do pretend work by putting on dress-up clothes and playing house or by piling all the blocks into a wagon and hauling them away to the "dump." You probably know that pretend play such as this helps with vocabulary and language development in general. But did you know that it also helps with reading? I don't mean that it helps with reading just because all oral language is important to reading and writing. Pretend play involves symbolism, and symbolism is what written language is all about. Symbolism is involved when youngsters pretend that a block is a telephone, that a scarf is a long skirt or a super-hero cape or that wooden beads on a plate is dinner. These experiences of symbolic representation enable a child to understand that marks on paper can be symbols for words, which in turn are symbols for real things or ideas.

Adventures and knowledge

Besides work and play, valuable learning experiences come from adventures. An adventure may be riding your new bike around the block, walking to the duck pond to feed the ducks dry bread or looking for pretty rocks and shells at the beach. Some adventures vary according to where you live and what kinds of experiences are available. My children grew up near a glacier that was constantly changing and near salmon-spawning streams that provided annual excitement. Your children may have access to orchards or corn fields, to snowy mountains or a seashore, to cool woods or prickly cactus. All are interesting and important to learn about. To little children everything is new and exciting. They are entranced by the self-serve gas pump, by road-repair equipment and by the array of fruits and vegetables at the grocery store. All these things can be part of an adventure.

The more of these experiences your child has, the more your child will know. And the more your child knows, the more prepared he or she will be to read and write. We all know you need to have something to write about. Even fiction writers build on their own experiences. Do you also know that you need to have experiences to give meaning to your reading? Researchers say that we must bring meaning *to* the printed page in order to get meaning *from* it. You can probably remember trying to read something totally foreign to your experience and background. No doubt you found it either *boring* or *too technical*. Like you, children enjoy

Everything is new and exciting to little children. Photo by Mary Mullen.

reading about those things they can understand through past experiences. Without this understanding, they may be able to say the words on the page, but they will not really be reading. Reading involves meaning.

The Importance of Experiences:
* Nurture thinking
* Encourage discovery of ideas
* Give meaning to reading
* Provide content for writing
* Are children's way of learning

Parental Guidelines for Intellectual Development:
* Encourage active rather than passive play
* Emphasize open-ended play activities
* Choose real things for play materials when possible
* Encourage your child's symbolic use of play props
* Let your child help with real work
* Take your child on errands
* Do not correct mistaken ideas
* Explore your surroundings with your child

Section 2

Your Infant Starts on the Road to Literacy

A walk with dad provides a change of scene and needed intellectual stimulation.

5

Defeating Boredom;
The Enemy of Learning

Everyone who meets 9-month-old Patrick remarks on how good natured he is. He's noted for being "such a happy baby." When he and his mother stayed with us for a few days, my teenage son observed with amazement, "He never cried!"

Although he does get frustrated sometimes, Patrick has little need to cry. His life is interesting and pleasant, filled with exciting new things to see, taste and touch. He isn't left in his crib to stare at the same old ceiling or plunked in a playpen with the same boring old toys. His parents, Katy and Mike, pay attention to his cues that he wants some *action*. They consider this an indication of his desire to learn, and feel sorry for babies whose parents ignore such signs for fear of *spoiling* them.

As a newborn, Patrick was prone to fussy periods, but Katy and Mike quickly figured out that taking Patrick for a walk made him mellow again. It was as if he simply got bored sitting around the house and wanted a change of scene. If this can happen to adults, why not to a 2-week-old?

Patrick's parents continued to experiment to discover what Patrick's fussing was about. They didn't believe that it meant nothing, but rather considered it an attempt to communicate his needs. Katy discovered that he responded well to interesting objects and pictures he could look at. So she started propping things up for him to see. It seemed to her that Patrick's active little brain felt trapped by the limitations of his uncoordinated baby body. Mike agreed, thinking how he would feel if he suddenly couldn't talk or make his body do what he wanted.

Learning by tasting

What Patrick really wanted was to put everything he saw into his mouth. As soon as he was able, this is exactly what he did. He especially loved to taste Momma—her cheek, her hair, her sweater, even her shoe. What lovely textures all wrapped up in the lovliest person of all! Patrick still leads with his mouth whenever he sees something interesting. He laughed with delight then opened his mouth wide when Katy showed him a colorful picture. He loved that picture and wanted to put it in his mouth.

All babies experience their world through their mouths first. This is their way of knowing or understanding things in their first stage of intellectual development. This is their way of getting knowledge about the world which is essential to making meaning of oral language and written language. When well-meaning adults try to protect infants from germs by keeping everything out of their mouths, a major source of intellectual stimulation is cut off and future learning has a shaky foundation.

New skills

It was a great triumph when Patrick was finally able to get his own hand or thumb into his mouth all by himself. He was beginning to have some control over his body. Katy and Mike didn't hand him everything he wanted, but rather encouraged his efforts to reach things for himself. How hard he would work trying to get his hand in contact with a set of keys. His eyes would be fixed on them with total concentration. His whole body would strain with the effort of making his hands move toward those enticing objects. This desire to learn and grow is so strong that we need to be sure and nurture it so it will last clear through his learning to read and write, and beyond.

We nurture learning and growth by not getting in the way. We should not do things for babies that they are trying to do for themselves, nor should we stop their exploration of the world lest we stop their striving to learn. Instead of the conservative approach to safety where we decide not to let our infants crawl around or touch something, we need to think about how they can be protected, but be safe and still explore. Katy knew that Patrick's new crawling skills would propel him fearlessly off the top of the stairway at my house. Because she didn't have a special protective gate with her, she decided

Patrick's parents don't hand him everything he wants.
Instead, they encourage him to reach things for himself.

to prop my ironing board on its side to cover the
stairway entrance. Of course dangerous objects
have to be moved from a baby's reach. Put
poisonous cleansers up high and any tiny objects
off the floor.

Have you noticed that babies practice inces-
santly as they master the fine motor skill of picking

up something between their thumb and forefinger? Developmental charts call this *the pincer grasp.* They practice by picking all the lint off the rug and, of course, eating it. Patrick gets to practice his pincer grasp as he eats Cheerios®, his current favorite finger food. Katy and Mike allow Patrick to use meal times for his intellectual development. He is not only allowed, but encouraged, to stick his fingers into his juice glass and feel the sloshy liquid in there. Lucky Patrick! His parents know he needs to explore with all his senses to learn about his world. They are willing to let Patrick learn baby things now and save lessons on manners for later.

Experiencing the world

As part of learning through all his senses, Patrick's bath times are special. He has a plastic circular support seat that helped him sit up safely in the bath even before he could sit alone. This frees his hands to splash in the water and see what happens. His mother trickles the nice warm water over his back and shoulders so Patrick can experience that sensation, while he chews happily on his wash cloth. Certainly Patrick's bath is a multi-sensory learning experience.

Patrick is very interested in the real world. Now that he is big, he can go for walks in his backpack instead of in the Snuggly® carrier. From way up high on his mom or dad's back he can see the world at adult level. He can see the faces of the people who stop to talk to his parents and to admire the smiley baby peering out of the pack. He can see all

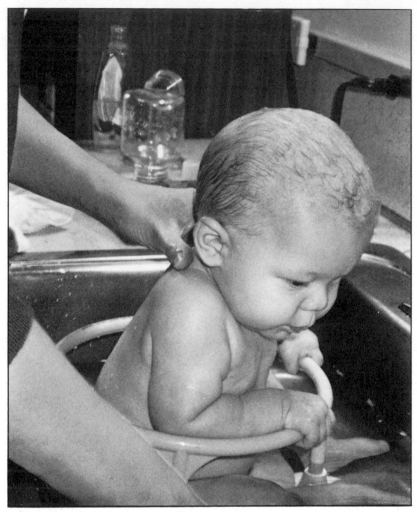

Patrick's bath is a multi-sensory experience.

bright objects on the shelves at the store and admire the colors of the trees and sky during a hike. What a wealth of information Patrick collects as he travels around in his backpack.

He likes to be part of whatever his parents are doing at home, too. When Mike or Katy are reading the newspaper, Patrick wants to touch and taste that newspaper. When they bring home papers from work, Patrick desperately wants to get his hands on those papers. He loves to play with paper of any kind; it makes such wonderful noises as he grabs it and chews it. His parents just keep an eye on him to be sure he doesn't get a wad in his mouth and swallow it. Katy and Mike understand that Patrick needs to explore real things, not just plastic baby toys, if he is to learn about the world. He not only needs to discover how paper feels, but also the metal of his backpack, the wood of the coffee table and even glass objects with supervision.

Part of joining in with adult activities is helping with housework. Already Patrick wants to be involved when Katy is filling the dishwasher with dirty dishes. Patrick can pull himself up to stand propped against the open dishwasher door and then pull the silverware out of the silverware holder as Katy puts it in. He is so engrossed in the work of manipulating the silverware and having such a wonderful time that Katy doesn't mind having to do some of her work over again. She says she has learned to plan on things taking lots more time with a baby around.

Quality time

Unfortunately, more time isn't always available. Many babies have two parents who work all day and who have little time to spend on household chores. In fact, both Patrick's parents are

Patrick's parents allow him to use mealtime for intellectual development. They know he needs to explore with all his senses.

teachers who are trying to balance their professional lives with their role as the center of Patrick's universe. They enjoy their careers and believe that they have more to offer Patrick as a result of the fulfillment from their work. But they do not have more TIME to offer Patrick. They know the old platitude, "It is not the amount of time, but it's the quality of time that counts." However, they also know it is hard to dredge up quality when you are tired at the end of the day.

Katy and Mike are still exploring a variety of approaches to achieving the balance between parenting and careers. Fortunately Patrick was born early in the summer when both parents were free. Then his father worked half time one semester and his mother worked half time the second semester. They also experimented with taking him to work occasionally. They didn't want Patrick with strangers when he was so little. When they do have child care for him, they make sure that person will treat him much as they do. First of all, they make sure that Patrick is with someone who sincerely enjoys his company. Secondly, they make sure that Patrick will be provided a stimulating environment while being kept safe.

Helping baby learn

Whoever Patrick is with and wherever he is, he will be gaining huge quantities of knowledge daily. There is so much to learn during this first year of life. Katy and Mike know that the best way to help Patrick learn and grow is to follow his lead. His interests and inclinations are the best indicators of what is appropriate for him to learn. They are aware that babies do not learn by directed instruction methods where the adults take charge of trying to teach certain things. They realize that Patrick's insatiable curiosity to touch and taste everything is the best evidence of how babies learn: through their own exploration. Katy and Mike laugh at the advertisements for flash cards

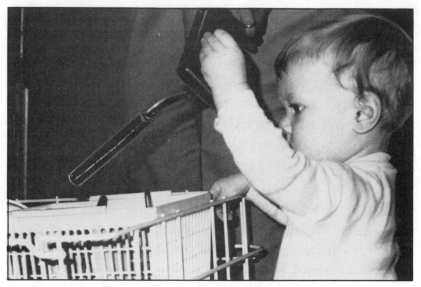

Patrick wants to help mom when she is loading the dishwasher. He busily takes things back out and examines them thoroughly. He is such an eager learner.

and other commercial materials for teaching grown-up lessons to babies. Patrick has a full educational schedule of his own.

How to Assist Your Infant's Intellectual Growth

DO

For a pre-mobile infant:
* Make interesting objects visible
* Carry your baby around to see things

For mobile infant:
* Make environment safe for exploration
* Find a variety of safe things for your baby to taste and touch
* Make interesting objects reachable
* Ignore manners at meals

DON'T
* Get too busy for your baby
* Confine your baby to a playpen
* Ignore cries for attention
* Be overly concerned about germs or tidiness

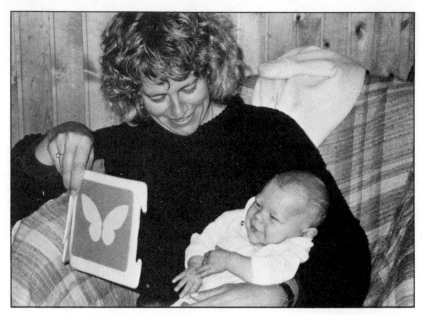

Patrick liked books and the sounds of language right from the start. Photo by Katy Spangler.

6

A Language-rich Environment

Patrick taught his Dad how to talk to babies: He paid attention when Mike talked to him in a high voice. The high pitch and repetitious language we commonly use with infants is called *motherese*. This is just one example of the ways parents naturally use exactly the right technique to teach language. Parents are natural language teachers. Yet they usually aren't even aware of their essential role in helping their children master the intricacies of speech. Furthermore, parents usually don't realize that these early language *lessons* start their babies off on the road to reading and writing.

Language lessons

Like your baby, Patrick apparently was born with an interest in language. He would pay attention to the sound of a human voice right from the start. Katy and Mike thought he paid most attention to their voices, because he was used to them before he was born. Mike had been talking to him through Katy's stomach just to make sure Patrick would

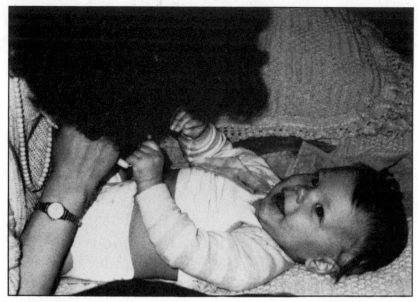

As Patrick gets a dry diaper, his Mom talks to him about what's happening. Patrick is learning about language in the process.

know his Dad's voice. By the time he went home from the hospital, Patrick was studying how people made those sounds. He would watch his mother's mouth intently as she rocked him and sang him nursery songs. Soon he was practicing by making little vowel sounds and moving his tongue around as he watched Katy's mouth. Like you, Patrick's parents delighted in every sound their baby made; they often played with him by repeating back to him the sounds he made. His responsiveness encouraged them to talk and sing to him all the more. As a newborn, Patrick was already getting the models of speech, the experiences of interactive language and the encouragement he needed to progress in his language studies.

Your baby's contribution to conversation goes from gurgles to coos and babbles. Photo by Debbie DeMars.

Katy keeps up a steady stream of language when she is caring for Patrick. She knows his language abilities are unfolding even though he isn't yet capable of creating words. She sometimes carries on conversations with him in which she answers for him. At other times she asks rhetorical questions that require no answer. "Are you my little darling?" she croons over and over as she picks him up and tends to his needs after a nap. "Does Patrick like to see Raggedy Andy? Oh Patrick loves his Raggedy Andy!" trills Katy as she helps Patrick enjoy his toy. These conversations are full of repetitions, which help babies to zero in on certain words. Researchers have documented this language-teaching behavior of parents around the world. They describe it as carrying on *proto-conversations*, which they say are part of *interactional scaffolding.* Isn't it amazing that you do these things without ever having heard of them?

Patrick's contributions to the conversations have progressed from an occasional gurgle to definite cooing and babbling. "Ahahah," chortles Patrick, and then adds, "goo ga." Sometimes he accidentally says, "mom" or "dada," and gets a great response from his parents. His ability to make sounds has increased rapidly with his maturation. He tries out these new abilities by playing with sounds. Katy says he seems to get special enjoyment out of the vibration of his lips as he says "vvvv." Your child may have a different favorite. Patrick has learned how to click his tongue, too, and loves to show off this feat. I remember when my son was that age. Clicking was a big thing. He started by clicking at the grandfather clock in the hallway; apparently his version of *tick-tock.*

Talking with baby

Katy explains things to Patrick and treats him like a real person even though he can't talk. She doesn't just change his diaper; she explains to him what is happening. This gradually helps him to learn the language associated with his daily routines, and is a way of treating him with respect. "Here comes Mommy to get her little darling. We'll make Patrick all nice and dry," Katy assures him. "Here is Patrick's new diaper," she adds as she lets him hold it for a minute. Katy may not be making a special effort to teach Patrick English, but she is making a conscious effort to make him feel good about himself. She doesn't want him to feel powerless; that things just mysteriously happen to him. Katy wants Patrick to grow up with a sense of control; that what he does and feels make a difference.

Like you and adults everywhere, Katy naturally limits her speech with a baby to the here and now. Language researchers call this *contextual support* for speech. The things Patrick is seeing and experiencing while his mother talks help him get meaning from the words he hears. When Katy holds up the Cheerios and suggests, "Patrick wants some Cheerios?" Patrick bounces his highchair with eagerness. He knows what his mother is talking about because he can also see what she is talking about. Hearing the names of things he sees and experiences in his environment—hearing them over and over—eventually helps him sort out which words go with which things.

Language games

One day soon he will be able to participate more actively in conversation by pointing to things as someone names them. This is clear evidence of a baby's ability to understand speech even though he's not yet able to talk. He will be able to find his toes and his belly button because of bathtub games identifying them. He will point to the Cheerios box when asked, "Where are your Cheerios?" You probably have played this pointing game and other language games with your own child. The universal peekaboo game is an example of what researchers call *routinized speech*. We start out doing all the talking ourselves, playing all the roles and answering as well as asking the questions. "Where is Daddy?" says Mike as he ducks out of Patrick's sight. "Peekaboo!" Mike exclaims as he pops back into view. Right now, all Patrick can do is laugh with glee. But as Patrick matures, Mike will encourage him to participate more and more. Eventually, Patrick will be able to instigate the game himself and recite the words at the proper time. This gradual increase in expectations seems to be a natural outcome of parent sensitivity to their children's language development.

Beginning communication

Inevitably, Patrick will also want to initiate conversation. Before long he will begin to direct topics to his own interests by pointing to what he wants to talk about. I am often surprised at how well youngsters can communicate through pointing combined with intonation. They can indicate through a questioning tone that they want to know what something is called. Or, through a demanding tone they let us know they want the thing being pointed at. When we observe babies communicating in this way, we can tell they already understand a lot about language. Even though they cannot create language as we know it, they are aware of its function as communication and they have a good sense of the general sounds of language.

Patrick has developed a fine sense of the give-

and-take quality of conversation, too. His parents make sure he is in on what's happening when people are talking, so he gets to observe the process and hear the sounds. Mike and Katy don't just leave Patrick on the sidelines. Instead, he is usually in the midst of whatever is going on. They even found a substitute for the traditional highchair that seats a baby away from the dinner table. Patrick has a seat at the table with everyone else. His little seat hooks on to the edge of whatever table the grownups are using. Although he can't form words, he definitely participates in the dinner conversation and obviously takes great delight in doing so.

Babies and books

Because reading is an important part of what goes on at Patrick's house, he gets in on that, too. Katy and Mike have been reading to him since he was tiny. At first he just lay in their laps, enjoying the cuddle and sound of voices he loved. Now he is actively interested in the books themselves. His enthusiasm requires sturdy cardboard pages which will stand up to his kind of interest. He likes to touch and taste books as well as look at them. He has progressed from randomly hitting at the pages in excitement to more sophisticated responses. Now he pats the pictures, shows pleasure in familiar favorites, turns the pages and jabbers at the pictures. It is obvious that Patrick already has an interest in reading and a significant knowledge about it as well.

Patrick's enthusiasm for books requires sturdy cardboard pages.

Sometimes his interest can be a nuisance, like when Katy wanted to finish a good book she was reading to herself the other day. Patrick wanted only one thing in the whole world—the book Mom had. But Katy doesn't mind too much because she knows that it is just natural for Patrick to want to do what he sees his parents doing. She knows he is developing a life-long love of books. Patrick will want to read as a result of seeing his parents reading and having them read to him.

Individual pacing

Some babies progress faster, some slower. Patrick is proceeding at his own rate along the road to literacy. He is learning how both oral and written language are a part of the world he lives in. He is motivated to learn about both language modes in order to fully participate in that world and interact with the people in it. He is using the learning strategies appropriate to his age as he works to unlock the mysteries of language. His parents are providing the models, the experiences and encouragement to help him learn, but they are letting him direct the learning. No "Superbaby" lessons with drill and flash cards or other artificial forms of teaching for Patrick. Katy and Mike are confident that he is progressing at a normal rate and learning what is important for him now. They are aware that normal development varies greatly and refuse to get involved in comparing baby accomplishments. Katy and Mike can tell that Patrick is learning as he watches and listens. They can observe Patrick's progress as he practices his perceptions of language and reading. They are sure that one day he will be able to read, write and talk with skill and confidence.

Encouraging
Infant Language Development:

* Use high-pitched voice in talking to your baby
* Use repetitious sounds in talking to your baby
* Talk about what is happening during diapering and feeding routines
* Play language games with baby such as:
    Peek-a-boo
    Where is your nose, tummy, etc.
* Expose your baby to adult conversations
* Read to your baby

Section 3

Your Toddler Becomes Aware
of
Reading & Writing

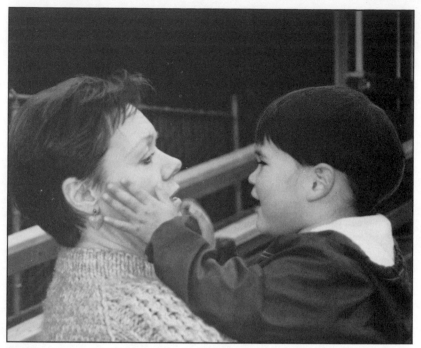

Teach your child language through meaningful in-depth conversations. Toddlers as well as adults rely on shared experiences to understand one another's language.

7

First Words

When youngsters start to walk, they begin to be called *toddlers* instead of *babies*. This transition generally coincides with the beginnings of language as we know it. Suddenly your baby is walking around and talking; increasing both skills at an almost alarming pace. When my first child began to walk, I suddenly realized—with mixed emotions of pride and dread—that he would one day be grown up and on his own.

Children at this age have an immense drive to be independent and participate in all that is going on. Margo says her 2-1/2-year-old son Jordan desperately wants to be big. Jordan insisted on getting rid of his diapers before Margo was ready to potty train him. He also gets frustrated that he can't do everything big kids do on the playground equipment. He is equally insistent on learning language. In just the past four months he has gone from only a few words to a large vocabulary. He tries out any interesting new words he hears, including "damnit."

How speech is acquired

We know that learning language is not just repeating what is heard. Speaking is a process of continually creating new sentences unique to the situation. Likewise, understanding speech is a process of comprehending the meaning of language unique to a situation. So, although your toddler may be a great little mimic, there's much more to the task of learning to communicate verbally. Current research has abandoned the theory that language learning is merely a process of imitation that results in sounds that adults reinforce through attention. Linguists studying language acquisition now describe an elaborate process of figuring out the system; a process common to youngsters learning any language in any country.

Your child is going through this same complex process. What you hear may sound like baby-talk and nonsense, but in reality it is study, practice and a search for understanding on a sophisticated scale. The toddler years are the time when your child learns to communicate; a major intellectual feat necessary for developing reading and writing ability. Children seem to love the challenge!

Beginning language patterns

I see 2-year-old Christy twice a week and her vocabulary seems to double each time I see her. She is proud of the words she knows and never misses an opportunity to tell me the names of familiar objects and events. I can usually tell what she is saying because she talks about what we are seeing and doing at the time.

Young children rely on these kinds of context clues both for others to understand them and for their understanding of others. You know how important it is to see what the child sees if you have ever tried to talk to a toddler on the telephone. I have spent many frustrating moments "talking" long-distance to a 2-year-old niece or nephew who just HAD to talk to Aunt Marjie.

If Christy and I weren't sharing a present experience when she talked to me, I would have to rely on her mother to translate for me. Debra knows Christy's personal version of the English language and can carry on in-depth conversations with her. Debra knows that "ca ca" means *cracker,* that "su sha" means *sunshine,* "yanya" means *lasagna.* Although these pronunciations are Christy's own, they reflect the same principles of simplification used by children everywhere. Like other youngsters, Christy avoids consonant clusters such as **cr** at the start of cracker, she is more interested in beginning sounds than ending, and she makes multi-syllable words as repetitious as possible.

Jordan is trying to tackle some longer words. "Heptopter" seems a valiant attempt at *helicopter* and "ca doo doo" is a reasonable facsimile of a rooster's crow. Notice that Jordan has cut off one or two syllables from each word and also reduced the number of different sounds in each. He is an expert at simplifying language during his learning process.

Parents simplify vocabulary for toddlers. Roses, violets and lilies are all called *flowers*. Photo by Debbie DeMars.

Importance of parents

Christy's mother shares with her a common set of experiences over time which also helps in understanding what Christy is talking about. For instance, she can respond appropriately to Christy's excited yell, "Nini!" when they drive by a certain store, because that is where their friend Nini works.

Jordan also assumes everyone knows what he knows. The result is that so often only his mother, father or grandparents have any idea what he is talking about. For instance, I am at a loss when Jordan tells me, "Go swimming in pool. I shiver—no." I need Margo to help me understand that Jordan is telling me about his upcoming visit to his Grandparents in Florida. His grandparents have a pool and he is explaining to me that it will be warm enough to swim outdoors. Parents have a definite advantage over care givers as teachers of language. No one but family can know so much about a child and, therefore, no one else can have the same quality conversations with a child.

Meaningful in-depth conversations with your child are the way you most effectively teach language. When you respond to a single word as if it were a complete sentence, answering appropriately, you are teaching a great many things simultaneously. Most importantly you are furthering your child's understanding of language as communication, which in turn makes language all the more enticing to learn. When Jordan remarks simply, "Kitty roof," Margo has sufficient knowledge to respond appropriately, "Yes, the kitty was up on the roof." With this response Margo validates Jordan's observations and his ability to communicate. She then goes on to extend the conversation and her child's language "lesson" by asking, "How did kitty get down from the roof?"

Of course Jordan's conversations with his parents also provide additional words to add to his vocabulary. Jordan is alert to specific words, but his job is hard because there are no spaces between words in spoken language. His parents respond to lots of "whassat?" questions, giving names to the important things in his environment. Margo and Vance also simplify for Jordan by using general terms such as *money* for all coins and *flower* for all kinds of blooms. This allows a toddler to communicate an idea without having to learn so many words or make so many distinctions. Jordan's parents are like most parents in naturally simplifying just the right amount for their child's level of development. They also limit their conversation to what Jordan can see and touch, and they use short simple sentences when speaking to him.

Sentence structure

Like toddlers everywhere, Jordan and Christy both use short *telegraph* sentences. For Christy "My bebe" can mean *Where is my doll?* or *This is my baby.* or *I won't go without my doll!* There is no mistaking her meaning, given the context and her tone of voice.

Jordan is trying to communicate more than a two- or three-word sentence can convey, so he sometimes strings statements together. In this approach, each *sentence* provides the context for the one to follow: "I swing. Back and forth. On tummy. Two owies. On a leg. I strong." Before long Jordan will be able to form complex sentences, but for now he communicates effectively to an attentive listener.

Talking with his parents also gives Jordan

models of the structure of English grammar. That doesn't mean he will necessarily put sentences together the way an adult would. Like all toddlers, Jordan is busily creating his own idea of how to put words together in sentences. But he knows the basic structure and always says, "Jordan wants juice," never, "Juice wants Jordan." Although he tends to get *me* and *I* mixed up, he has figured out the subtle difference between *my* and *I*. He can say "My glass" or "I go."

Christy is still working on that concept saying, "I appo" for *My apple*.

Jordan is currently trying to figure out how to form negatives. "I cry—no," and "I tip over—no," are his latest versions of *I didn't cry,* and *I won't tip over.* In a conversation with him recently I happened to say, "I don't have it any more." Jordan echoed, "No more." This is a perfect example of how children hear only what they are ready for. He changed my words to match his perception of negative-statement forms, as well as shortening my sentence to a length he could manage.

Baby talk

Your toddler shares some of the sound substitutions that Jordan and Christy use. The sounds of L and R are so difficult that Jordan's words "wadder, pwane and dwives" are common versions of *ladder, plane and drives.* It seems too that little kids always say "fink" for *think.* Many sounds are difficult for young children to form. Time for maturation rather than criticism or special lessons will

Physical development influences which sounds a child can produce. Substitutions for the **L**, **R** and **S** sounds persist into the school years.

remedy these normal immature language patterns.

Fortunately, neither Christy's parents nor Jordan's parents think they should correct toddler language errors. This is consistent with language-acquisition research: Correction of errors in pronunciation or grammar has no positive influence on language development. Children do the best they can according to their level of maturation. Physical development influences which sounds they can pronounce. Intellectual development influences their perception of how they should pronounce words and put sentences together. Parents assist language learning best when they accept the communication intent of what children say, responding to the meaning instead of to the form.

Language models

Jordan goes to his Dad and says, "Hurt self." Vance answers, "Did you hurt yourself? Where does it hurt?" After Jordan shows off his skinned knee, Vance has the information to say, "You hurt your knee." Then he asks, "How did you do that?" He clarifies this question by adding, "What were you doing when you got hurt?" This father, like most, instinctively responds to the meaning of his child's words and gestures. He also restates what his child says in complete sentences; this is called *elaboration* and is important for providing a model of adult language for children. In this response Vance also asks questions that give Jordan prompts about further appropriate explanations. Through this casual exchange, Jordan is learning much about oral-language sentence structure and about communication strategies. Most important, Jordan is learning he can communicate and that what he has to say is valued. This kind of feedback encourages children to continue exploring the rules of oral communication.

When parents engage their toddlers in large quantities of in-depth conversation, responding to what they say, elaborating on their simple sentences, and overlooking their errors, they are being effective teachers of language. Children with a rich background of oral language will have a firm foundation for relating to written language.

Talking With Your Toddler:

✳ Accept your child's simplified pronunciations
✳ Engage your child in frequent conversations
✳ Generally limit talk to the "here and now"
✳ Elaborate on your child's abbreviated sentences
✳ Show interest in your child's comments
✳ Respond to your child's questions
✳ Do not correct your child's language errors

8

Learning & Doing

Christy is always on the go. Her dad says she is in the *search-and-destroy* phase. Nothing is safe from Christy now that she can climb and reach things previously out of harm's way. She gets into her big sister's treasures, spreading chaos and destruction in her wake. Door knobs and cupboard latches no longer stop her and she is constantly in danger of tasting or touching something dangerous. Sometimes she drives her mother, Debra, to distraction with her insatiable urge to explore and find out about the world around her. Debra can't seem to get any work done or a peaceful minute to relax.

Christy is a normal toddler. Her description probably fits your toddler perfectly. Because you don't dare turn your back on a toddler for a minute, you might as well decide to enjoy, encourage and channel all this activity. Thinking about how much your little tornado is learning will be a big help to your enjoyment. Remembering that your child's experiences are the base for language development

Toddlers quickly become bored with their toys.
They have an insatiable urge to explore the
real world and learn about it.

and thinking skills, you will be more willing to put
aside your work and assist with your child's equally
important work.

Diversion Tactics

Debra is becoming a master of distraction and
diversion techniques. Whenever Christy goes after
something off-limits, Debra tries to divert her.

A plastic tub of sand or water can provide hours of
satisfying play and learning for a toddler.

Debra looks for diversions that offer a similar at-
traction, but are safe from and for a toddler. Big sister has been taught this same diversion technique
for self-protection.

Planning the environment for a toddler is a big
help. At Christy's house, the higher shelves on the
bookcase have grown-up and big-sister books;
lower shelves have books for Christy. To keep her
from causing trouble with the operator by playing
with the real telephone, she has a realistic play
phone of her own. The stereo buttons and equipment are a *no-no*, but Christy has her own record
player with sturdy plastic discs that make music.
Many drawers and cupboards in the kitchen have

childproof locks on them, but Christy is free to explore the plasticware and the pots and pans in others. Debra knows that Christy needs materials that allow her to imitate adult behaviors as part of learning about the world.

Diversion also involves prevention activities such as setting up water-play for Christy so she won't be so insistent on playing in the toilet-bowl water. A plastic tub of water on the kitchen floor can keep Christy involved for more than her usual one-minute's concentration. Debra varies the accessories so one day Christy has a funnel to pour water through, another day a strainer, and other times just various sizes and shapes of containers to pour back and forth between. Of course Christy also drinks the water, but it is clean and so is the floor after Debra mops up the water Christy spills. Christy not only begins to learn about the nature and properties of water, she also is soothed and relaxed through water-play.

Another soothing material for toddlers or older children is soft, squishy, homemade play dough. Children love to squeeze it, roll it, pound it and—when they're older—shape it. Christy has her own container of play-dough tools: a toy rolling pin, plastic cookie cutters, and wooden popsicle sticks to cut and mark the dough. It just takes a few minutes to make up a batch and it keeps well in the refrigerator, especially with a little alum in the recipe. So Debra can make sure Christy always has access to play dough. When she is feeling very patient, Debra lets Christy help make up the mixture.

Homemade Play Dough

1-1/2 cups water
1/2 cup salt
2 tablespoons oil
2 tablespoons alum

Food coloring of your
choice
2 or 3 cups flour

Mix 1-1/2 cups of water with 1/2 cup of salt. Add to mixture 2 tablespoons of oil and 2 tablespoons of alum to make mixture keep longer. Mix in any food coloring and add 2 or 3 cups of flour. Knead until no longer sticky.

Store mixture in a plastic bag in refrigerator when not in use.

Such a help

Although it will be another year or so before Christy can get involved with cooking projects, Debra gives Christy a bit of the dough to work with when she bakes, lets Christy sample ingredients as she makes salads or allows Christy to help with stirring. Of course Christy wants to do everything she sees her mom or dad or big sister doing. So she washes toy dishes in her water-play tub sometimes, and has her own toy broom and dust pan. Naturally, she would rather use the big broom, which endangers everyone and everything as the long handle swings wildly above Christy's head. Outside where there is more room, she is allowed to use the lightweight snow shovel. She feels very important as she works at clearing snow off the walk.

One task Christy is very good at is dusting. She can safely use a dust cloth and actually is good at cleaning those low surfaces adults have a hard time getting to. Another job she loves, but which is of dubious help, is cleaning the front of kitchen appliances with a sponge. Debra allows this activity, but recently she barely caught Christy in time before she used the kitchen sponge to clean the toilet. Such a help. But Christy feels grown-up and useful and so her self-esteem is growing in the positive directions which will assist her success throughout life.

Getting out of the house

Although there is much to explore and much to do at home, Christy's intellectual development also requires exposure to more of the world. Debra has chosen to be a full-time mom, so she is at home with Christy all day. This means that Debra also has a need to get out and see more of the world. To keep them both from getting bored at home, they go off on an adventure almost every morning. They talk about what they are doing and Debra notices how Christy's vocabulary grows with each outing.

An outing needn't be exotic to be an adventure for a toddler. Simply going along and helping on errands can be wonderful learning expeditions. Of course they are only wonderful if parents plan on the errands taking two or three times as long as without the child. Otherwise, it is only a lesson in frustration for both parent and child.

Christy is excited to be going on an outing. Her vocabulary
and knowledge grow as she goes places with her parents.

A toddler learns much from a visit to the pet store. Maybe she will even get to hold a cuddly bunny.

When Debra takes Christy to the post office, she lifts Christy up so she can pull down the bin door and drop letters in by herself. Then she takes time to allow Christy to explore the rows and rows of post-office boxes with their fascinating key holes. Christy insists on having a key and she checks box after box trying to get Debra's car key to fit into one. Christy is also interested in the people waiting in line to mail packages and would love to get behind the counters. She points and jabbers about the activity she can glimpse behind the scenes when her mom lifts her up. When Debra has to wait in that line herself, she prefers not to take Christy along. She knows better than to expect a toddler to wait patiently, but she takes Christy whenever she has the time. She knows these experiences are essential to Christy's intellectual development and her language development.

When Debra has an errand in the mall, she and Christy always stop for a visit at the pet store. Christy is learning the names of the animals now, though at first she said "bird" when she saw the fish swimming in their tanks high above her head. It is fun to watch her dance up and down with excitement when she sees the puppies cavorting in their cage. The expression on her face is priceless as she watches the parrot turn somersaults on his perch, using his beak alternately with his claws to hold on. She gets the experience of watching the parrot hold a peanut shell in one claw while daintily picking out the nut with his beak. She gets to see the gerbil running around on his exercise wheel and

Exploring outdoors is an important activity for intellectual development.

shows her understanding by saying, "Whee!" What a rich experience base for relating to picture books about animals! Fortunately, the pet-store owners are hospitable, even when Christy picked up a bag of peanuts for the parrot and spilled them all over the floor. Christy even helped to pick them up—for a minute.

Playground equipment allows toddlers to test their growing coordination and strength.

The great outdoors

Exploring outdoors is a favorite activity for both Debra and Christy. A toddler can find adventure in his or her own yard. Grass, weeds, gravel, puddles, leaves; everything is new and interesting to a very young child. Of course she has to watch what Christy is putting in her mouth, but Debra finds it peaceful when they stroll around in their own yard or in a nearby park. Christy loves to point and name the things around her as she practices her new power to symbolize her experiences with language. Debra need only affirm or expand with comments such as, "Yes, that is a rock—a flat rock," or "Christy found a flower? Is it a pretty flower?"

At the park there is playground equipment with which Christy has been gradually testing her increasing coordination and strength. She likes to walk over and under the small wooden bridge and she climbs on the lower portion of the climber. The slide is a special challenge to her. It took her awhile to climb up the ladder, each try getting farther before she asked mom to take her down. Finally after watching other children for awhile, she decided to slide down. Debra is right there in case of emergency, but encourages Christy's expansion of skills. "Christy slid down the slide!" Debra congratulates Christy on her achievement as she catches her at the bottom.

These kind of simple and accessible activities are essential ingredients for your child's developing literacy and for his or her intellectual growth. This is the type of education your child needs at this point—and you are the perfect teacher. Another important benefit is the joy you and your child share and the bonds you create as you spend special time together. The investment is small and the rewards are great.

Experiences and Materials for Toddler Learning:
* Going for a walk
* Playing at the park
* Exploring in your yard
* Visiting the pet store
* Going on errands such as:
    The post office
    The gas station
    The grocery store
* Helping with housework or cooking
* Exploring kitchen pots and pans
* Using and helping make play dough
* Water play

"I wrote my name!" Photo by Marilyn Holmes.

9

Wonderful Scribbles

You may not be exactly overjoyed when your toddler scribbles on the wall. Debra wasn't thrilled either when she discovered blue crayon marks covering a large portion of the white paint in the hallway. But then Christy looked up at Debra proudly and said, "I wrote my name!" How can anyone be cross when faced with such an irresistible smile? Christy was giving Debra an important message: I am ready for writing materials.

Accessible writing materials

Providing paper, crayons and markers for your tot will save your walls as well as assist in the important work of a beginning writer. Toddlers who see big people writing want to write, too, just like they want to do everything else you do. Their babyish attempts at writing will be as comical and inept as their first attempts at walking or talking. When babies begin the process of learning to walk, they stagger, crash and show little grace. Similarly, when they begin the process of learning to write, it is uncoordinated and experimental in nature.

At first, Christy can hardly even keep the crayon on the paper, let alone make marks resembling what we call *writing*. Debra puts generous quantities of newspaper around the blank paper for Christy's writing; this protects the table from the crayon. Debra emphasizes the idea of writing only on the paper by sitting down beside Christy and writing on a piece of paper herself. She also explains to Christy that we write on paper, not on walls, floors or furniture. This means that lots of paper has to be available and accessible to Christy. Debra and her husband Louis explore sources of free scrap paper such as newsprint roll ends and used computer paper. The backs of junk mail and even the envelopes provide another source of paper which is replenished daily by the mailman. This paper, along with crayons and washable markers, is kept on a low shelf in the living room where Christy can help herself. This keeps her from improvising on the walls if Debra or Louis are too busy to help her when Christy is in the writing mood.

Encouraging writing attempts

Now when Debra writes a letter to her brother, she is often joined by Christy writing a letter of her own. The fact that Christy's letter is written entirely in scribbles doesn't keep it from being included in the envelope with Debra's. This makes Christy feel big and a part of the literate society around her. Because your child needs to see you write to begin

Christy's scribbles are similar to her baby talk; uncoordinated, but the begnning of her use of written language.

the process of understanding why and how we use writing, don't put off writing that letter until after the kids are in bed. Even though it may take lots longer, go ahead and let your toddler climb on your lap while you make out the grocery list, too. Your use of writing provides important lessons in literacy.

Christy's scribbles make Debra think of her babbling and cooing baby talk; both are uncoordinated efforts at using a form of language. Debra is good at encouraging the beginnings of oral language *and* of written language. She pays attention to both and responds to the communication intent, despite the primitive form. Just as she talked and smiled and goo-gooed back at Christy's babbles, Debra admires, asks about and displays Christy's scribbles.

Magnets on the refrigerator are great for quick displays, but also consider a display board down low where your toddler can easily see it. Displaying their writing and art work lets youngsters know that it is important and keeps them interested in doing more. A chalk board can also encourage writing and drawing if it is easily reached and especially if it is located where parents and a big sister write on it, also.

Building competence

With practice, Christy's scribbles gradually become more controlled. They still don't look like writing or anything else recognizable, but the marks stay on the page and Christy is beginning to realize that the way she moves her hand and the crayon or marker is related to how the marks look. Finger-painting and brush-painting activities help with this realization and with the coordination necessary for eventual control. Debra mixes up powdered tempra paint with liquid starch to make a thick paint that is washable. Christy can use this for either kind of painting. Often Debra just lets her finger-paint on a plastic tray instead of on paper

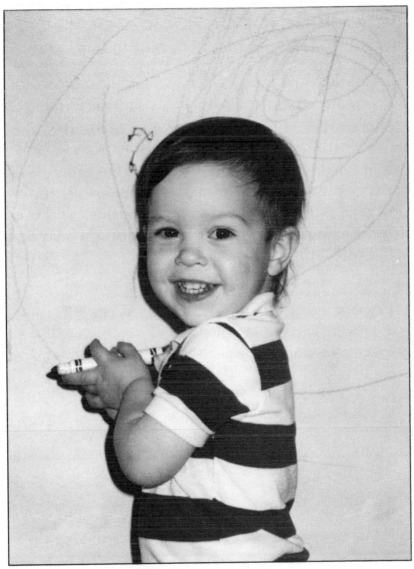

Scribbles are the beginnings of purposeful representation.

because Christy doesn't care about a finished product; she is interested in the process of moving her
fingers around in the paint and seeing the results.

Christy's writing and drawing look the same right now. They are only different in her intent: If she says she wrote a word, it's writing; if she says she made a picture of Mommy, it's drawing. Most often there is no distinction yet because this age child rarely scribbles with a product in mind. Sometimes scribbles are named after they are made, as the child decides the marks look like something. Scribbles are the beginnings of purposeful representation. Children need to be cherished and nurtured to help them grow into important ways of self-expression.

Encouraging Your Toddler to Write:
* Provide accessible materials
* Let your child see you writing letters, lists, etc.
* Encourage your child to write with you
* Accept any marks your child identifies as writing
* Display and admire your child's work
* Provide for eye-hand coordination practice

10

Please Don't Eat the Books

Children who are read to become readers. If you didn't begin reading to your child in infancy, toddlerhood is the time to begin. Children can understand, enjoy and become fascinated by books during their second and third years of life. My son Michael had borrowed *The Little Fire Engine* from the library so often by the time he was 2 that I bought him his own copy for his second birthday.

The value of storytime

When you read to toddlers, you provide important assistance with learning language. You allow them to observe what reading is and you start them on a life-long love of books. The lively language and matching illustrations found in children's books enrich a young child's vocabulary and expand his or her horizons. In addition, watching closely as Mom or Dad or Sister reads is a way of obtaining significant information about how to read and what reading is. Probably the most important aspects of storytime, however, are the cozy

When you read to your toddler, you allow him to observe what reading is. This starts him on a life-long love of books.

feelings of togetherness and focused attention of parent with child. These good feelings become associated with books, making reading an attractive pastime.

Storytime can also create an oasis of peace in a hectic day with a toddler. When Christy is getting into everything and making a nuisance of herself, Debra will often drop what she is doing and suggest a storytime. This option gives Christy two things she craves; her mother's attention and some intellectual stimulation. Good books can put some excitement, interest and food-for-thought into a toddler's otherwise humdrum day.

Choosing books

A book can either be an experience in itself or it can recapture an experience for a child. *Pat the Bunny* is an experience in itself with the invitation to feel the furry bunny picture or smell the flower picture. Bright, bold pictures and the ingenious format of *The Very Hungry Caterpillar* make that book another experience for toddlers. A book needn't have holes in the pages or furry pictures to be an experience. The simple, satisfying plot and straight-forward pictures in Lenski's *The Little Fireman* certainly created a satisfying experience for Michael.

Jordan is attracted to any book featuring construction machinery. He has been watching a major excavation and road-repair project near his home and greatly admires the "big diggers." For Jordan, books about bulldozers, backhoes and trucks recapture and build on an exciting experience. These books help him think about what he has seen. When he looks at pictures of the machines, he names each one and works at telling what it does. In his own way, he is reading these books. In the process he is improving his language skills.

Jordan also loves books about cats. Having a pet cat makes these more meaningful. Margo is now looking for books about squirrels since Jordan

Books are a natural part of life for Jordan. Everyone in his family reads books.

became interested in them during a recent walk. When she was asking the librarian about squirrel books, she was shown a reference book called *Subject Guide to Children's Books in Print*.

Books are a natural part of life for both Jordan and Christy. Everyone in their families reads books and owns books. They each have a special low shelf for their books. The ones they have been just been using are spread around the coffee table with everyone else's. Both children have special favorites among their books that they frequently bring to their parents, asking to be read to. Jordan and Christy can pick out specific books upon request, too. "Go get your Dirty Dog book," says Debra, and Christy will sort through all her books to find her much read copy of *Harry The Dirty Dog*.

When to read

Storytimes aren't reserved for bedtime routines; storytime can be any time. Although a story can help with winding down for a nap or a night's sleep, Margo notices that Jordan interacts with his books more when he is awake and alert. She can understand that easily because she doesn't get much out of the reading for her college classes when she is tired. Debra hasn't made a ritual out of bedtime stories for Christy, either. She tried that with her older daughter and found out that the ritual removed all flexibility from bedtime; Hanna expected a story no matter how late it was or how tired everyone was. So for both Jordan and Christy, storytime can be any time. The important thing is that storytime occurs frequently and is high-quality time—high quality of interaction between child and book, and between child and parent.

Different books, different approaches

Parents of toddlers can learn from their children how best to share books with them. Tune in to your child's responses and you will be able to tell what approaches are effective. Different approaches are useful with different children, with different books and at different times. Jordan loves his book of trucks and machines by Richard Scarry, but he doesn't want it read. He likes to point and name the pictures, taking great delight in learning the names of the great variety of things Scarry packed into the book. When he can't identify

Some books have short, simple stories that a toddler can easily follow. Others need to be paraphrased or simplified.

something, he asks, "What's dat Mommy?" Margo doesn't particularly like this book's cartoon pictures, but she bows to Jordan's preferences.

Jordan has other books that have a plot, and he enjoys having stories read to him. When they read

Corduroy, Jordan says, "What happens?" as he helps turn each page. He picks up the comment as a result of Margo's questions of "What do you think will happen?" when they read stories. Some books have short simple stories that a toddler can easily follow; others need to be paraphrased or simplified. On some days Jordan wants Margo to read; other days HE wants to "read." Then he proceeds to tell the story in his own words, turning pages carefully and using the pictures as prompts.

Christy is still more interested in reading pictures. She loves her *I Can—Can You* books, delighting in doing all the tricks portrayed in the simple pictures. She has enjoyed *Max's Toys* for quite awhile and enjoys showing off her ability to name all the pictures in this book. It's a good thing this book has reinforced and laminated pages so it can withstand Christy's devotion. The simple plots of *Sam's Bath* and *Sam's Cookie* are just right for her when she is ready to listen to someone else read. These books portray familiar everyday situations toddlers can relate to. Both youngsters respond well to *I'll Love You Forever,* but their mothers had to read it over and over before they could read the ending without crying. Normally we wouldn't read a novel to a 2-year-old, but Christy seemed to enjoy *Little House on the Prairie* when her mom read it to her big sister. She snuggles on mom's lap and listens contentedly to the stories her fourth-grade sister loves to hear.

Wordless picture books allow youngsters to make a story their own and adapt it to their own level as well. *Sunshine* and *Moonlight,* both by Jan

Omerod, are favorites of Jordan's. Of course he also likes *Truck.* Christy delights in the small Mercer Mayer wordless books, especially *Ah-Choo!* Although Debra admires all of Peter Spier's beautiful books, she knows she needs to wait awhile for Christy to be ready for the detail of *Noah's Ark.* For now they enjoy Peter Spier's *Rain,* a book very well suited to the climate where they live. Toddlers enjoy reading pictures and, being basically oblivious to print at this point, will read most any book as if it were wordless. Jordan can tell you the basic story of *Peter Rabbit,* turning the pages of the small Beatrix Potter book at just the right times.

Rhyming books generally have great appeal at all ages. *The Napping House* is a favorite at Christy's house, sending Christy, her big sister and her mother into gales of laughter as they see the progressively more ridiculous situations shown in the quality illustrations. Jordan and his parents enjoy reading *Over in the Meadow* enhanced by Rojankovsky's lovely illustrations. Vance just found a version illustrated by Keats, another favorite children's illustrator. It's hard to decide which one they like better. Many old favorite nursery-rhyme and Mother Goose books have been produced in beautifully illustrated versions. The appeal of these classics is ever-enduring.

Another thing that seems universal: Young children want repetition. For parents who are tearing out their hair at reading Dick Bruna's *Snuffy* over and over day after day, Dr. Bruno Bettleheim offers reassurance that children will move on to something else when they have gotten all they can

110

from a certain book. It is certain that your child gets much from books and story time.

When you take the time to introduce your child to literature at an early age, you have made a major investment in his or her education.

Good books for toddlers:

* *Ah-Choo*
* *Corduroy*
* *Harry The Dirty Dog*
* *I Can—You Can*
* *I'll Love You Forever*
* *Moonlight*
* *Pat the Bunny*
* *Peter Rabbit*
* *Rain*
* *Sam's Bath*
* *Sam's Cookie*
* *Sunshine*
* *The Little Fire Engine*
* *The Napping House*
* *The Very Hungry Caterpillar*
* *Truck*

Authors and illustrators to look for:

* Ezra Jack Keats
* Lois Lenski
* Mercer Mayer
* Jan Ormerod
* Feodor Rojankovsky
* Richard Scarry
* Peter Spier

Good books for parents:

* *Read Aloud Handbook,* ©1985, Jim Trelease, Penguin Books, New York.
* *Parent's Guide to the Best Books for Children,* ©1988, Eden Ross Lipson, Times Books, A Division of Random House, New York.
* *Choosing Books for Children,* ©1986, Joan Oppenheim, Barbara Brenner and Betty D. Boegehold, Bank Street Book by Ballantine, a Division of Random House, New York.

Section 4

Your Preschooler
Gains Understanding of Print

Brianna's mom faithfully recorded each of Brianna's new words as she learned them. But soon the sheer quantity of words made the task impossible. Brianna and her mom read the list in Brianna's baby book.

11

An Explosion of Language

Brianna's mom faithfully recorded each of Brianna's new words for as long as she could, but soon the sheer quantity of words made the task impossible.

It is average for a 3-year-old to have a vocabulary of 1000 words. With this arsenal of words, a preschooler is ready to take on the rule systems of the English language.

Accepting immature speech

Three-year-old Alex is working on how to pronounce and combine language sounds: "thix, theven" he counts as he stacks blocks for a tall tower. Alex can also be heard to yell, "bwast off!" His parents aren't at all concerned about the sound substitutions, because they know it is common for children to substitute for the difficult S, L and R sounds even after they start school. Alex's parents never attempt to correct his pronunciations because they know that maturation time and continued example is all that he needs. They know what Alex is saying and they enjoy talking with him.

Alex is also working to understand grammar. "Then them go home to them Mommy and then them take a nap for a little bit," Alex says as he explains his version of a storytime favorite. Carol listens attentively and doesn't correct her son even when he continues, "Them falled in some water." She merely exclaims, "They fell in some water?" With this response, Carol acknowledges Alex's communication and at the same time models the correct grammar.

Carol recognizes Alex's creative grammar as his efforts to make sense of the rules of his language. She knows that this is just a phase that will soon pass because that isn't the language pattern Alex hears all around him.

Additionally, no one prompts Alex or makes an issue of it when he seems to stutter, "Wh-Wh-Where's my hat?" He has made a hat at his child-care center and is worried that it is missing. His teacher helps him find it and calms his fears without mention of his brief *non-fluency* (stuttering) experience. Judy is aware that this is normal for 3-year-olds; their minds race faster than their ability to speak, sometimes causing a stutter-like effect.

Judy follows the same guidelines for assisting language development in this case as with all other immature language patterns. She pays attention to the *meaning* rather than the *form* of the child's language. She never says such things as, "Slow down and try it again." Judy's background in child development taught her that calling attention to normal non-fluency can cause a more serious fluency problem or at least hinder a child's confident exploration of language.

How quickly they learn

At 4-1/2, Brianna has a much more sophisticated language ability. Her fluency, pronunciation and grammar are basically adult. She is gaining skill with semantics as she uses her language knowledge to combine words differently and convey subtle variations in meaning. She is able to construct elaborate comparative sentences such as "The hummingbird is smaller than all of them." She can communicate in detail, as when she explains, "I can't read it because the letters are sort of different." Brianna continues her quest for knowledge about language. She asks questions such as, "What's out-active?" in response to her Dad's explanation of the terms *active* and *inactive*.

Brianna is also becoming skillful in matching her speech to the social interaction context. As another child picks up one of her beloved dinosaur books, she informs him, "That's my book . . . but you can read it if you want to."

While helping in the kitchen, Brianna politely asks her father, "Could you get me my own special knife?" Her gracious offer to give me "a kiss and a hug" as I left her house showed her understanding of my attitude toward her and was appropriate. Each of these exchanges accomplished her objective because she was able to express herself in an

Language proficiency comes with practice. Playing house is a good activity for language practice.

assertive, yet pleasant manner fitting the situation. This important language skill causes people to respond favorably to her communication efforts.

Practice makes perfect

How do children attain such language proficiency in so short a time? Like so many things in life, it comes with practice, practice, practice. You may notice your preschooler practicing. Most parents say they couldn't wait until their children talked, but soon wished they would stop for a few minutes.

Just like any of us learning a new language, young children need to actually use language in a give-and-take situation to learn it. The conversations your child has with you provide important language practice and effective language lessons. The structure of a conversation with Mom lets Alex know if he has been successful in expressing himself. Carol's response tells Alex whether or not she understood what he is trying to say. She indicates whether he needs to explain more or whether he can continue with what he is saying. Recently he was trying out a new word and checking it with his mother. "This tape is unusable," Alex said in disgust as a wad of tape clung to his fingers instead of the paper. "Yes it is. It's all stuck together and you can't use it," Carol replied, validating his statement. But when he looked at a picture of his baby cousin and stated, "Adrianne is unusable," his mother contradicted him. Through her laughter Carol said that she didn't think Adrianne was unusable. Carol's response is typical of how mothers effectively teach language. They correct errors of fact, but not errors of speech itself.

Carol's knowledge of Alex's experiences helps her understand what her 3-year-old is talking about, just as it helps Margo figure out her 2-year-old's language. Shared context continues to be an asset throughout a child's language-acquisition period. Shared context was certainly necessary the day Alex suggested, "Hey Mommy, let's play All Play." At first Carol had no idea what he was talking about and said, "I don't know what you mean." So Alex tried again, "At Uncle Curt and Aunt

Alex's mom was with him at the fire station. Her knowledge of his experiences helps her understand his speech when he talks about putting on the fireman's suit.

Susie's," he explained. Then it dawned on Carol that he was referring to playing *Pictionary* at a relative's house four months previously. Alex had picked up the term *All Play* from the game and

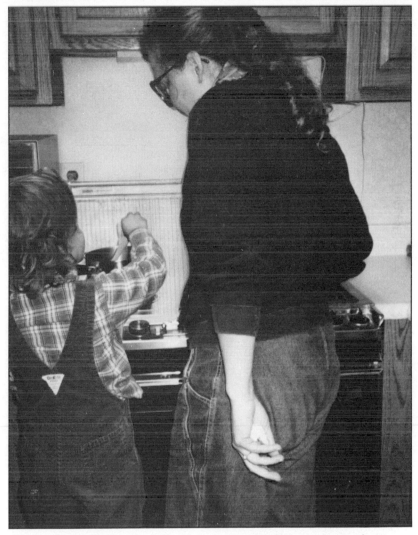

Shared activity provides an opportunity for conversations between mother and child. Language lessons are a fortunate side effect of shared times like these.

remembered it. Carol was able to figure out what her son was talking about even when he dredged up an event from four months earlier. He wasn't yet able to indicate past tense or provide sufficient information for someone who hadn't been there. Talking to someone who understands what you are trying to communicate is obviously much more encouraging than the opposite experience. If we meet with frequent failure, most of us stop whatever it is we are doing. Parents and others who know a child well are more likely to provide success experiences with language. Therefore, those close to a child are the best ones for talking practice.

How parents teach language

Talking is an *expressive* language skill; hearing and understanding what others are saying is a *receptive* language skill. Children need practice with both—and conversations provide practice with both. When Phoebe talks to her 4-year-old daughter, Monique hears how language sounds and gets to practice making sense of it. Phoebe simplifies her language somewhat for Monique, but doesn't limit herself to sentence structures and vocabulary that Monique herself has mastered. Phoebe realizes that children can understand much more than they can say, and that they grow in their understanding by hearing a little more than they already know. Just as she talks to Monique's baby brother, even though he doesn't yet talk, Phoebe uses future and past tense, and other grammatical structures that Monique doesn't yet use.

Phoebe doesn't think about teaching language as she talks with Monique, rather it is a fortuitous side effect of their shared time together. As parents

Talking with a puppet is good practice for language development.

tune in to their children, giving them respect and attention, the naturally ensuing conversations provide exactly the right language-learning opportunities. Phoebe doesn't think about teaching the rules of conversation any more than she thinks about teaching the rules of grammar, but she is teaching them anyway. When we look at someone who is talking to us and take turns in talking, we are following the rules of conversation. Children learn both grammar rules and conversation rules by being involved in conversations. Experiencing a large number of conversations is the only way to learn to converse.

Phoebe *does* think about the kinds of questions she asks Monique. She tries not to ask too many of the kinds of questions people usually ask young children such as: "What color is your dress?" or "How many toes do you have?" She attempts to avoid questions with one- or two-word answers, right or wrong answers, and especially questions she already knows the answer to. Those questions limit conversation. Instead, she strives for questions that open up conversation and represent honest communication rather than a testing of knowledge. She especially likes questions that involve Monique in thinking creatively, such as "What do you think would happen if . . ." Other good conversation starters are "I wonder how . . ." or "Tell me about . . ." There is an amazing difference between responses to "How was school today?" and "Tell me about school today."

Sometimes Monique doesn't want to talk; Phoebe accepts that response, too. She knows that demanding a response will only be counterproductive in the long run. Phoebe's intent is to let Monique know her mother values her as a person and is interested in her ideas. Knowing this, Monique feels safe and confident. She is then willing to talk and try out her emerging language skills, whether they be oral or written.

Assisting Your Preschooler's Language Development

DO
* Listen carefully to understand your child
* Provide models of good speech and grammar
* Carry on conversations with your child
* Ask thought-provoking questions
* Enjoy your child's communication with you
* Spend time with your child

DON'T
* Worry about mispronunciations
* Correct *creative* (immature) grammar
* Make an issue of stuttering
* Ask questions you know the answers to

Preschoolers learn how to interact with literature. They make hypotheses, form questions and react to what is read.

12

Read it Again

Just as you are teaching about oral language whenever you talk with your child, you are teaching about written language whenever you read to your child. You probably can't imagine how many important literacy concepts are shared during a cozy storytime. Your purpose in reading to your child is most likely to share a pleasant time together and maybe to entertain your youngster. Your focus on the pleasure of reading makes your incidental teaching all the more powerful.

Learning to read from storytime

You may want to know what your child is learning during storytime even though you would not want to conduct *lessons* on these topics. Previously, I mentioned the important attitudes about reading that come from being read to. I also explained how Christy and Jordan are learning about what reading is during storytime. Preschoolers continue to develop attitudes and understanding about reading, but are now working on more sophisticated concepts about written language and books.

Preschoolers are learning strategies for understanding an author's meaning. One such srategy is relating book content to relevant past experience. Another is drawing inferences from print and pictures. They are also learning how to interact with literature: making hypotheses, forming questions and reacting to what is read. Preschoolers are still learning about what reading is, only now they are noticing more detail than when they were toddlers. Some of the detail involves beginning to pay more attention to the words, realizing that it is not just the pictures that tell the story. Let's look at examples of how children learn these things.

How parents teach with stories

When Carol reads a story to Alex, far more than half of what she says is commentary rather than direct reading from the text. The first time she and Alex read about *Curious George,* Carol asked many questions to find out if Alex understood such as, "Who is George?" and "Why did the firemen come?" When she discovered any confusion, Carol was able to clear up misunderstandings with additional explanations. Carol helped Alex understand what was happening to George by encouraging Alex to compare George's experiences with his own. Alex could understand about being in deep water and not being able to swim because he had been swimming. He knew about such things as helium balloons because he'd had several of his own. And he

Alex knows a lot about fire engines from his collection of fireman books. He can identify much of the fire-fighting equipment.

knew about monkeys in the zoo because he had visited the zoo.

While helping Alex understand this one story, Carol is also helping him learn how to make sense of stories in general. Researchers suggest that parent-child storytime conversations help children make sense of written language in the same way that general conversations help children make sense of oral language. Remarkably, most parents just naturally interact with their children in the most effective manner for teaching both kinds of language competency. In addition, parents naturally match the amount of their story interpretation to children's maturation and knowledge. How nice that we can do our best teaching merely by enjoying our children and sharing a good book with them.

After Alex was familiar with the story and the Curious George character, Carol's questions during subsequent readings focused on keeping Alex actively involved with the story. Her approach is to encourage Alex to create a personal meaning for a story. "How do you think George felt when he was caught in the bag?" Carol asks. This helps Alex to identify feelings and to relate to the main character. A question such as, "Should they have put George in jail?" encourages Alex to think creatively and value his own ideas. Carol contrasts this interactive approach with the passive response encouraged by television viewing. She emphasizes books while deemphasizing television in Alex's life.

Why parents are excellent teachers

In deciding what questions to ask and what understandings to check, parents rely on knowledge of their children's past experiences. They also con-

Children often study a storytime favorite as they try to figure out the match between written and spoken words.

sider their children's level of development. Parents are best able to figure out what a child is talking about because of their information about the child's context of experiences. Similarly, parents are the ones best able to match storytime conversations to a child's own experiences and understandings. There is good reason for early childhood experts to say that parents are a child's most important teachers.

When Phoebe reads *The Little House* to Monique, they can talk about Monique's own experiences with cities versus the country. Phoebe can also help Monique think about her own reactions to the changing seasons. Due to intimate knowledge of her child's life, Phoebe can also help Monique compare her own feelings about a recent move with the little house's feelings about moving to a new place. Phoebe shares her own personal response to the story by exclaiming, "How awful," when the little house is cut off from the sun by tall buildings and expressways. Phoebe is modeling an interactive approach to reading at the same time she is helping Monique learn how to make sense of a story.

Phoebe's tone of voice, facial expression and gestures as she reads also help Monique make sense of a story. Phoebe tends to point to pictures of things she is reading about, such as the trolley cars and the elevated train going by the little house. This is one way to help Monique know what the words mean. Phoebe gives further clues to meaning by showing through her voice and in her face the emotions proper to the passage being read. Her voice and face were very different when she was reading about the little house surrounded by ugliness and when she was reading about the little house being back in the country surrounded by flowers. Even Monique's baby brother, who often listens in, can get some sense of a story through these nonverbal clues.

Stories for individual needs

Just as you automatically adapt your speech to your child's level of understanding, you probably adapt stories the same way. You may skip over long descriptive parts of a book that do little to further the plot. You probably also simplify and shorten stories too sophisticated for your child's background or attention span. Phoebe finds it is better to tell the story *Sylvester and the Magic Pebble* than to read it. She and Monique talk through the story together as they turn the pages and get clues about the content from the pictures. However, Monique can sit through the entire 68 pages of *The Story of Ferdinand*. Brianna's parents thought they would have to adapt the beautiful but long story of *Mufaro's Beautiful Daughters* when they read it to her. They were pleasantly surprised that the compelling folk tale, lavishly illustrated by John Steptoe, held her attention completely.

Brianna is at the stage of trying to make a match between the print and the words read. At this stage, it is helpful to share books that can be read verbatim so a child can work at following along. Brianna still gets much meaning from pictures, so it is important that the pictures compliment the text. You may have noticed that youngsters get very upset if a picture seems to contradict the story.

Make Way for Ducklings, an old favorite, does an especially nice job of matching pictures to the story. McClosley's clear drawings capture each aspect of the plot. Alex likes this story a lot because of his experience feeding the ducks at a pond near his house. He can use this experience to make personal meaning of the book; but at the same time the book also adds to his understanding of his experience. Carol is delighted at how much similarity there is between the pond in the story and the

Alex uses his experience of feeding ducks at a pond to make personal meaning of the book *Make Way for Ducklings.*

pond by their house: both have an island in the center, both have a paved pathway around the pond and both have wild ducks nesting there that follow people around for food. She is hoping that there will be baby ducklings in their pond this Spring, too. If there are, Alex will have more understanding about the ducklings he sees because of reading the book.

Books can also help children better understand what they are feeling. Like so many 3-year-olds, Alex's new level of imagination has resulted in fear of the dark and bedtime. He is very interested in stories about monsters and children with fears like his. He frequently asks Carol to read *There's a Nightmare in My Closet* to him. He seems to get reassurance from hearing the story and from the subsequent discussion of his own fears. Carol was looking for more books on fears and got a book list from the child's librarian that lists books by topics such as *New Baby, Moving, Death,* etc.

Choosing books

The local children's library is an important part of Carol and Alex's life. They go to the library for children's story hour every Friday, at that time checking out new books and returning last week's selections. Carol works a four-day week so she can spend more time with Alex. She has chosen story hour day as her day off. She and Alex are very careful in their book selections, looking for attractive pictures as well as interesting stories. Carol knows that if a book appeals to her, she will be more able to share it well with Alex. However, she looks for a well-developed plot and colorful language to keep Alex's interest and doesn't let herself be swayed merely by beautiful pictures. She often tries to find books recommended in the *The Read Aloud Handbook* by Jim Trelease or other reputable sources such as *Parent's* magazine. Alex's preferences are the bottom line, though. The books are for him and must please him.

Carol and Alex also check out nonfiction books on topics of interest to Alex. He is entranced by fire engines, so they frequently check out both fiction and nonfiction books on that topic. Carol thinks that they may need to check out nonfiction books about ducklings and eggs hatching soon. Alex is learning from her example that books are an

Alex and his Mom go to story hour at the library every
Friday, at that time exchanging last week's selections for
new books.

important source of information.

Brianna is mainly interested in books that are
a source of information. She prefers her dinosaur
books over those with plots. She has accumulated

a vast store of knowledge about dinosaurs. She amazes adults with her ability to identify all kinds of the reptiles and even pronounce their names. Her Dad says that Brianna's preference for fact over fantasy extends to her television viewing. Her favorite TV program is *Nature*.

Whatever the topic of the books, parent-child storytime is vital to helping a child become socialized to print. Doing this is vital to helping a child make sense of written language and becoming a reader. You know your youngster is excited about reading when you finish a story and get the request; "Read it again!"

Reading to Your Preschooler:

* Discuss the book together
* Relate stories to your child's experiences and feelings
* Interpret a story where needed
* Ask "thinking" questions about plot and characters
* Share your own responses to what you are reading
* Read with expression
* Adapt stories to attention span and understanding
* Encourage examination of print as well as pictures

13

I Sure Said Lots of Words

Reading isn't just confined to books, of course. Children encounter written language wherever they go in our literate culture. Road signs, store signs, advertisements, phone directories, menus, calendars and grocery lists are all part of their everyday experience. Experiences with these many kinds of print are important to a child's understanding of reading and writing just as are story books. It is probably obvious that exposure to print in the environment helps your child understand the various ways that reading and writing are used. Close observation also shows that your preschool child is beginning to use these written language samples to figure out the mechanics involved in reading and writing.

Reading basics

Children learn to talk through real conversation and they learn about books from real stories. They also learn more about print when it is used for real-life purposes than when it is presented in a lesson. Most preschoolers are not ready to master the skills of making and reading print. But they are very capable of understanding the concepts of why and how written language is used. Recent research provides evidence that this understanding is the foundation upon which literacy skills must be built. We now know that the *basics* of reading are not the ABC's, but rather interaction with written language. Even the precocious early reader needs these experiences to continue to grow. Brianna shows signs of becoming an early reader, but her parents want to be sure her learning is based on a firm foundation.

Brianna's Dad, David, helps her use print in her activities rather than teaching her letters and sounds. David knows that letters and sounds have no meaning in themselves and are much harder to learn in isolation. Besides, he wants Brianna to think of reading as having meaning rather than as making the sounds of letters. He wants to help her avoid what reading expert Kenneth Goodman calls *barking at print.*

Meaningful experiences with print

For the most part David doesn't have to go out of his way to provide experiences with print for Brianna, he just includes her in his activities such as shopping, cooking or following directions to put a bike together. Written language is so much a part of life, he doesn't have to search for teaching opportunities. Naturally, it takes more time and patience to make muffins with Brianna's help, but

"How many bananas do we need?" Brianna is learning to read as she checks the muffin recipe.

David thinks it's worth it.

First, they shopped together for the bananas, kumquats and other ingredients to make the muffins. This involved the literacy activities of looking up the recipe, writing down the things they didn't already have at home, reading the list once they got to the store, and finding the items in the store. Brianna now knows that kumquat starts with a K. She also is more aware of how helpful it is to write down things you want to remember; they might have forgotten the muffin-cup liners.

The recipe has to be checked again once the actual cooking begins. "How many bananas do we need?" David asks as he shows Brianna the recipe card and points to the numeral beside the word bananas. This way Brianna can "read" the information needed for the task. She follows up with counting out four bananas, peeling them and slicing them. Next, she reads that one cup of white flour is needed and begins to measure it. "Do you know where the one is?" inquires David pointing to the numerals on the side of the measuring cup. Brianna finds a **1,** but David shows her that it is part of **1/2** rather than a **1** by itself.

Brianna is having a meaningful experience with print. But, as with most really valuable education, this is an opportunity to learn many other things at the same time. Brianna's experience enlarges her understanding of the world and enhances her oral language development, too. As she pours the flour into the bowl, Brianna runs her fingers through it commenting, "This is really soft; very soft *and* white." Her Dad suggests that she contrast the white flour with the whole-wheat flour they will add next. Brianna declares whole-wheat flour "not as soft." David prompts, "What's the opposite of soft?" and Brianna comes up with "rough." Next they measure out the margarine and Brianna, having just learned that my name is Marjorie, exclaims, "That almost sounds like your name!"

Context clues

Brianna could read the grocery list, parts of the recipe and the word *kumquats* at the store. This was because of the situation or context in which the words appeared. Kumquats themselves were

Cooking provides a meaningful experience with print. It enlarges Brianna's understanding of the world and enriches her vocabulary.

evidence of what the sign above them said. Brianna knew the content of the recipe and the grocery list, so needed only small cues to remember or figure out the words. She wouldn't be able to read these words just anywhere, but was successful in these contexts. Brianna is having beginning reading experiences at the stage of contextualized print.

If you have travelled to a country where a language you don't understand is spoken, you probably have learned to read in the same way. My first Spanish word in Puerto Rico was *Salida* as we searched for the exit from the airport. Driving around the island quickly taught us to read other signs with messages such as *one way* and *road narrows*. Searching for a restaurant taught us to read *closed* when it is on a sign in a door. I found I could read the messages as long as they were on a sign with pertinent clues around, but I couldn't recognize the same words elsewhere. I suddenly had a much better understanding of children's reading of contextualized print.

Think how much easier it is to read a foreign language when it is written in a symbol system we already know. If I had been driving around Japan, I would have had even more understanding of what it is like for young children. They don't know the significance of all those squiggles. Initially youngsters have as hard a time telling the difference between letters of our alphabet as we have with Japanese characters. Considering that, isn't it amazing that 3-year-old Alex can identify the word **STOP** whenever he sees it on red road sign? Given the international nature of the Golden Arches, both American and Japanese children probably learn to read that sign equally early. Alex even referred to a **W** as an "upside-down golden arches."

The power of print

Alex knows a great deal about print already. He can read his name on his shoes, on his paintings and by his coat hook at the child-care center. He knows that his name on things establishes his ownership that won't be disputed. When confusion arises at the child-care center about whose boots are whose, he knows to check inside for a name. He asked Carol to put his name on his backpack, too, so that it wouldn't get taken home by someone else. Lately he has been trying to write his own name. His teachers respect his way of writing his name and have learned his unique signature. Carol was thrilled with Alex's signature on her Mother's Day card.

Carol helps Alex to notice the print in his world. Like David, she doesn't confuse learning to read with learning the alphabet. Instead of pointing out letters, Carol shows Alex things such as the sign on the library door that tells what day and time story hour is. She helps him notice the note at the child-care center reminding parents about the field trip on Friday, too. Then Alex "reads" the notice to her every day until the trip. Alex is learning that

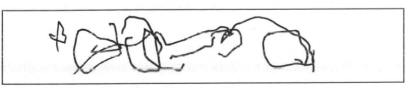

3-year-old Alex's signature. Children's understanding of how to write their own names evolves in distinct ways. This occurs at a faster pace than their general knowledge of print.

Watching someone write down what you say is an important part of learning to read.

written language can be an important source of information.

Print as a substitute for oral messages is another concept preschoolers learn through experience. Monique sees Grandma Kay and her Mom leaving notes for one another when their busy schedules get in the way of face-to-face communication. Phoebe sometimes leaves a note about a change in her work schedule that will affect mealtimes or child-care arrangements. Both Kay and

Phoebe write down phone messages for one another, too. Monique notices these things and also starts leaving notes. Her notes generally contain little more than a picture or a heart symbol, but they still demonstrate her understanding of notes as a means of communication. Kay and Phoebe don't write notes to one another in order to teach Monique about written language, but she learns from it anyway. This is another way literate adults socialize children into a literate society. As reading and writing are a part of your life, they will become part of your child's life.

Literacy lessons

There is a way you can help your youngster bridge the gap between understanding the purpose of print and being able to master it. You can be a "secretary" and write for your child. Transcribing a child's thoughts provides a powerful literacy lesson. Alex is used to dictation experiences both at home and at his child-care center. In both places, he can find an adult who is willing to write down just exactly what he wants to say. Carol knows that she must not correct his grammar in the process or else the ideas will not be in Alex's own words. She understands it is an important part of his learning that he see his language written just as he says it. Alex watches intently as she writes and listens with delight as she reads back to him what he said. "I sure said lots of words!" he boasts proudly. Alex is learning that what he thinks or says can be written down and can be read by others. This is a major

A fox and a hound falled in a chair and falled in some water. Falled in a car. And then they got out of the car and then them falled in a coat. It was a brown coat. It get them in the eye. Then them go home to them Mommy and then them take a nap for a little bit and them falled in a lunch box and thats all.

Alex C.

This is the story Alex dictated.

concept of literacy.

Alex generally dictates made-up stories influenced by books read to him. One story was about a fox and a hound he had seen on a TV movie advertisement. Sometimes he just likes to play with words to see them written down. Monique's creation of stories through dictation has given her a sense of authorship. Grandma Kay helps her make little books out of her dictation. They write a title and the author's name on the construction-paper cover, then staple it to the story. Monique is proud to have her name listed as an author. She is beginning to notice the names of authors in her story books.

Brianna is noticing the mechanics of writing as she watches David write down the information about dinosaurs she is dictating. David sits so Brianna can see how and what he is writing. He is careful to make letters uniformly so Brianna can recognize them. He also involves her in the writing process with decisions about where you start to write on a page, what you do when you come to the end of a line and whether or not there will be enough room to write *Archaeopteryx* on the rest of the line. David sometimes asks Brianna what letter she thinks a word starts with because he knows she is beginning to figure out the sound-symbol connections. Brianna can read what she has dictated because it has personal meaning to her and she can remember it. In the process of this memorized reading, she is learning to actually read some words so that she will recognize them out of context.

The children described here have not mastered all the minor skills involved in reading and writing. But because they are heavily involved in their literate society, they are learning the essentials of literacy. They are comfortable with print and know that it has purpose in their lives. They are eager to learn more about this useful tool and will work hard at becoming literate themselves. They are building a firm foundation for continuing to learn more.

Some Preschool Reading Lessons:

* Noticing road signs and store signs
* Seeing you get information from notes, menus and lists
* Using a recipe to help cook
* Using a grocery list at the store
* Seeing his name on his belongings
* Watching an adult write down what she says
* Hearing an adult read back what he or she dictated

14

What Does It Say?

Has your preschooler ever filled a page with squiggles and then proudly showed it to you and asked, "What does it say?" Phoebe wasn't sure how to answer when 3-1/2-year-old Monique first asked this question. Monique seemed so sure that it must say something. After all, she had made marks just like her Mom and Grandma do when they write. She knew adults could read writing and this obviously was writing. Actually, it looked quite a bit like writing to Phoebe, too. Loops and zig-zags were carefully drawn in neat lines across the page, very much like adult cursive writing.

Accepting early writing

"What do you want it to say?" might be a good answer if you are faced with this question from your child. This answer indicates that writers decide what they will write. For a child, this is an important piece of information about writing. This answer also suggests acceptance of the child's intention without judgment of the outcome. If chil-

Has your child ever filled a page with squiggles and proudly asked, "What does it say?"

dren's lack of knowledge about letter formation and spelling keeps them from experimenting with writing, they lose out on valuable practice. Your encouragement and reassurance about their efforts are essential to the courage and confidence children need to embark on this new learning adventure.

When you turn the question around, you can find out a great deal about your child's understanding of print. One child may simply respond, "I don't know." Another might reply, "A letter." While yet another could "read" in detail from the

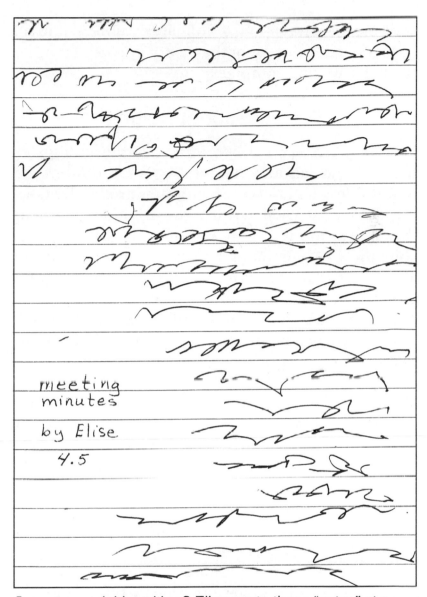

meeting
minutes

by Elise

4.5

Can you read this writing? Elise wrote these "notes" at a
meeting she went to with her mom.

scribbles. Each response indicates a different level of literacy development that is not apparent merely from the writing samples.

Teaching about writing

The first reply above indicates the youngster has little idea about what writing is for. If Monique is at this level, Phoebe can help her growth by talking about her own writing to Monique. She can think "out-loud" about needing to write down something to remember it. Or, she can tell Monique about her plans to write a letter to a friend. She might even find the time to write out a little story about an event in Monique's life and read it to her. These activities would help Monique begin to understand the purposes of writing.

These same activities would be helpful if Monique says her writing is just "a letter." Phoebe can tell from this answer that Monique knows at least one purpose for writing: She will want to reinforce this knowledge and expand it. One way she can increase Monique's understanding is to ask Monique to tell her who the letter is for and what it it says. These questions indicate to the child that writing has an audience and that it contains specific information. Mailing the letter to the intended recipient and getting a reply offers a priceless educational experience which makes a child feel very important about writing.

If Monique is specific about what her scribbles say, and if they are a coherent expression of an idea, Phoebe knows that Monique is already

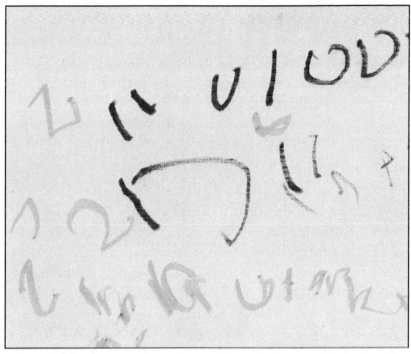

The author of this writing is very specfic about what this says: "I will buy you all the diamond rings and necklaces in the world."

literate in a certain sense. Young children's physical ability to write lags behind their ability to conceptualize writing. Many youngsters have good knowledge of literary style and can create a story with a beginning, middle and end; yet they cannot yet put these ideas into print by themselves. These children may know many of the conventions of writing, such as writing in lines from left to right and using letters; but it takes awhile to fill in the details and to make small fingers do as bidden. Later, Monique reads her page of scribbles to Grandma Kay when she comes home. If she reads it with the same message as before, Phoebe and Kay will know that Monique also understands that once something is written down, it stays the same. This is a major breakthrough and more evidence of progress in literacy.

Whatever her level of understanding, Monique does not need any direct *teaching* to help her improve. She needs continued exposure to people who read and write and talk about what they are doing, especially if they enjoy it. She needs people to be interested in what she writes and to take time to talk to her about it. She needs someone to answer her questions without giving her more information than she is ready for. Her mother is taking college classes, and so Monique sees Phoebe reading and writing and revising her writing. Once when Monique *read* a page of her scribbles, she said, "Oh, I don't want it to say that!" She then erased a line and rewrote it, subsequently reading it differently. This knowledge of revisions in writing will help her significantly as she continues to grow as a writer.

Influence of school

When her friend Nicholas comes to play, Monique likes to play dress-up, she likes to play with clay and puzzles, and she likes to get out her writing materials. Nicholas doesn't write long stories and letters like Monique does. He always asks to look at an alphabet chart or a picture dictionary when he writes. He limits his writing to copying letters and words, working very hard to form each

Drawing and painting are important steps toward writing.

exactly right. Of course this is very difficult, so he erases a lot and gets tired quickly. Phoebe notices a strange thing: His letters have big dots decorating them all over. When Nicholas' dad comes to pick him up, Phoebe asks him about the dots. He laughs and explains that at Nicholas' preschool they give the children worksheets on which they are to connect the dotted lines to make letters. Now Nicholas thinks letters are supposed to have dots! Phoebe is glad that Monique goes to a preschool without worksheets.

Jason goes to the same preschool as Monique, but he is 4 and this is his second year there. Last year his parents thought he would never do anything but play "super hero" up on top of the climber. Marilyn and Jim have two boys older than Jason who both seemed more interested in reading and writing, so they were a little concerned. They asked the teacher if Jason should be forced to do something other than large-muscle play at preschool. Linda has taught preschool for quite awhile and has seen this pattern before. She wasn't worried about Jason at all and reassured his parents that he was doing what was important for him. This year proves her right. Finally he is interested in the paint easels, puzzles, books and the writing center. In fact he spends a lot of time at the writing center.

Pride of authorship

Jason has so much he wants to write. It seems like he must create stories in his head as he plays and now they come tumbling out. He tells the most

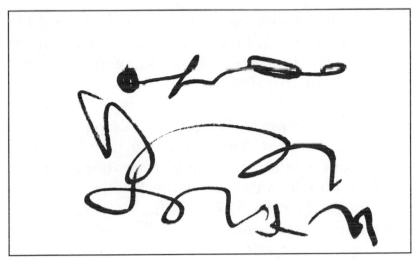

Jason's ability to write is still pretty primitive. But he is working hard at learning and enjoying every minute of it.

wonderful action-packed stories, just like the ones he loves to act out. Of course, what he writes on paper and what he means to say are not the same. Jason's ability to make letters and figure out how to make words are still pretty primitive. But he is working hard at learning and he is enjoying every minute of it.

He finds appreciative audiences for his writing both at school and at home. His little sister is very impressed when he reads his stories to her, his older brothers pay some attention and both parents are enthusiastic. No one but Jason can read his writing because he writes with letter-like forms and no sound-symbol relationship, yet he can remember days later exactly what he wrote. The illustrations that accompany his stories are another form of symbolic representation, allowing him to record his ideas in a form more easily understood by a child. Pictures can look a little like what you are trying to say, but letters seem to have no relationship to anything. Drawing is an important step toward writing for many youngsters.

Both Monique and Jason are making excellent progress as writers. They are eager, confident and knowledgeable about writing. I just hope no one comes along and destroys all this by showing them how much they don't know. This is often done in the name of *education*.

Encouraging Your Preschooler to Write:

DO

* Show uncritical interest in any attempts at writing
* Encourage your child to tell you about what his or her writing says
* Discuss your own writing with your child
* Provide models for writing through storytime
* Facilitate mailing and receiving letters for your child

DON'T

* Make an issue of correct letter formation
* Make an issue of correct spelling

15

Let's Pretend

Kids just naturally play. Even young animals play. Play is how they learn about the world and how they practice skills to function in it. A lot of learning was going on when Alex, Brianna and their friends pretended "pizza parlor" at the child-care center. It all started with making pizza from play dough and soon included tables and chairs, and a kitchen in a make-believe restaurant. There were even waiters and waitresses taking orders from customers. Of course they had to write down what kinds of pizza the customers wanted and read it to the cook.

Literacy lessons in play

Playing pizza parlor is an example of how youngsters seek to understand their experiences through acting them out. Going out for pizza was an experience these children had in common, so they could collaborate in acting it out. The social interaction involved in this play enhanced the children's social and language skills. As so often

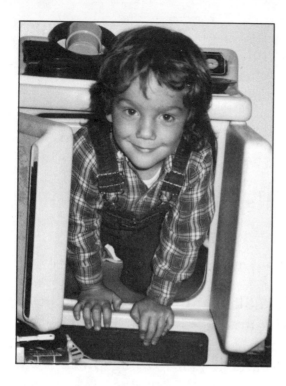

Props children use for dramatic play involve *symbolic representation*—an important concept for reading and writing.

happens, this play also fostered attempts at reading and writing. Additionally, the props used involved symbolic representation practice for reading and writing, as explained in Chapter 4. To the casual observer, "playing pizza parlor" might look like a lot of fun and no more. But those who study children's play assure us that intellectual, social, emotional, language and academic skills are being developed through play such as this.

There are many types of play, each with its own special benefits. "Pizza Parlor" is *dramatic play*. The most common form of dramatic play is "playing house." Many preschoolers have a pretend stove and sink or other playhouse props at home. Such props are standard at preschools and child-care centers. Children learn even more about symbolic representation when they create their own props, such as when they use a block to represent a cake in the oven. Playing house allows children to act out their most common life experiences and to try out the roles of the important people in their lives, Mom and Dad. Parents often cringe when they hear their own words coming from their child's mouth.

Feeling confident through play

At home Brianna likes to involve her family in pretend play where they switch roles. She thinks it is fun to have Mom pretend to be Dad and Dad pretend to be Mom. She also likes to pretend she is Mom and Mom is Brianna. Right now with her daddy out of town, she wants Mom to pretend to be Daddy. Then Brianna runs and hugs "Daddy" and tells him how much she missed him. When Brianna decides her family will switch roles with a friend's family, even the family cat is involved. Not only does Brianna become Chelsea and her parents become Chelsea's parents, the cat has to be Chelsea's dog.

Brianna's parents wisely allow her to direct this play. When they allow her to control a make-believe environment, they also assist her feelings of competence in general. Make-believe can counteract the feelings of helplessness that so often come from being too little and too young to do so many things. I frequently suggest parent

When children are allowed to control their make-believe environment, they gain feelings of competence.

involvement in child-directed pretend play as an antidote for unacceptable behavior. When my son Michael was a preschooler, he used to play that he was Underdog and I was Sweet Polly Purebred (from a cartoon on TV). Michael would plot terrible fates for Sweet Polly daily. All I had to do was yell, "Help Underdog! Save me!" Then Mike would punch a monster or stop a speeding train and be the hero. He got a great deal of satisfaction from this game. This experience helped me to under stand the value of fantasy play to meet some of the power needs of young children.

What does all this have to do with reading and writing? Emotional development is inseparable from intellectual development. An unmet emotional need will get in the way of learning. That's why earlier I mentioned Katy's respectful treatment of Patrick to help him feel important right from birth. When Debra allows Christy choices in her life, that is also contributing to intellectual development through meeting emotional needs. With preschoolers, their natural interest in *let's pretend* can help meet emotional as well as intellectual needs.

Defining play

Sometimes parents have trouble giving up control and want to direct the dramatic play themselves; then the value for the child is gone. In fact, play is no longer play if it is prescribed by someone else. The definition of play involves self-selection and self-motivation. The attitude of the person

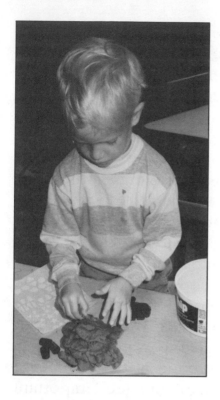

Children stay interested longer when they are involved in activities of their own choosing. This helps to increase attention span.

involved determines whether an activity is work or play. You may love to work in the garden and find it relaxing and pleasant to do so. For you gardening is play. For someone who is weeding a garden his wife planted after he told her it would be too much trouble, gardening is work!

Brianna loves to play around in the swimming pool and is making some progress at getting ready to swim. For her, swimming is fun. She has a friend whose parents insist on her taking swimming lessons that she doesn't want. This child doesn't get to mess around in the water. Her swimming time is directed by someone telling her to put her face in the water when she doesn't want to. This child may never find pleasure in swimming. For her, swimming is work. Many of us consider typing work. It may be what you do for a living. But Alex chose to type. Even though he was using an old manual typewriter that was hard to type on, I saw him persist with typing for over an hour. For Alex, typing was play.

The tendency to persist in an activity is a characteristic of play. When children are involved in activities they choose, they stay interested longer. This gives great practice in concentration and helps increase children's attention spans. Young children have a reputation for not being able to pay attention to something very long. If you watch closely however, you will notice that children have a short attention span for activities selected by an adult. But they are often engrossed for long periods in doing things they select themselves. A lengthened attention span is just another benefit of play that assists youngsters with academic success.

Monique was thoroughly engrossed with her blocks for a long time. She was building a miniature playground with a slide and a merry-go-round for some imaginary babies. Then she built a crib with four sides and added a roof on to "keep the monsters out." She was combining dramatic play with block play. Creating things from blocks, clay or other raw materials is called *constructive play*. But dramatic play and constructive play often trigger one another. Play dough started the pizza-parlor play and the imaginary babies started Monique's block play.

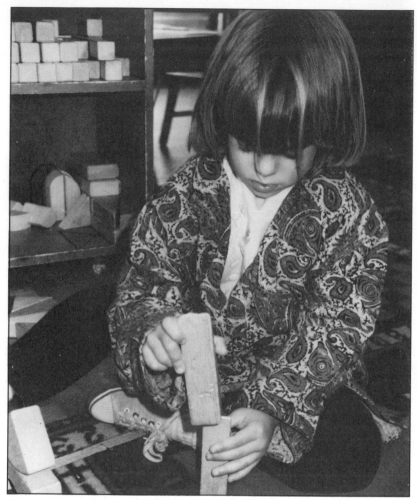

Play solves the problem of matching children's activities to the task. Open-ended material such as blocks allow children to select the right challenge and skill level.

Efficient learning

The structures Monique created are simple ones. She is matching her use of the blocks to her own level. An older child might come along and create something quite sophisticated with the same materials, but each would be exploring and learning at a personally appropriate level. That is another beauty of play. Play has no right or wrong way until you get into games with rules. Play frees children and adults alike to take risks without fear of failure. Play solves the problem of matching children's abilities to a task. When a child self-selects an activity and decides how to proceed, that child can be counted on to select the right challenge and skill level. The playful non-threatening experimentation with materials and activities creates attitudes and ways of thinking that are useful learning tools. Research shows that play experiences assist with problem solving and creative thinking abilities.

Young children learn more through play than they do through direct instruction. Play is not only a more pleasurable way to learn, it is a more effective way for young children to learn. The waiters and waitresses in the pizza parlor play were learning far more about reading and writing by using it in play than if they were matching letters and sounds in a workbook. Similarly, you can help your child learn better by facilitating play than by trying to teach.

Parents and play

Renowned child-development expert Bettye Caldwell says that the most important foundation for children's healthy development is the mutually pleasurable play between adults and children. Playing with your child can be a great source of pleasure to you and your child. The pleasure and the joy of being together is the primary benefit; the educational value is a bonus. You will notice that children are more drawn to adults who are willing to play with them. I can't help but wonder if we might make a life-long difference in the quality of our relationship with our children through play in the early years. Will a preschooler you play with become a teenager more likely to interact positively with you?

If you want play times with your youngster to be pleasurable, you need to be sure and keep them light. Guard against typical adult tendencies to impose rules and to view play as a means to an end. When Brianna tells a friend at the slide, "No cut throughs!" she is dealing with rules for play at the preschool level. Preschool children are not ready for games where someone wins and everyone else loses. Preschoolers all need to win. Wise adults keep playing lotto until everyone's card is filled. They also play musical chairs without removing a chair each turn.

Although you don't want to direct play or impose your ideas about play on your child, you do have much to offer in play. For one thing, your attention and interest stimulate play by showing that you value it. Just your presence during play is likely to keep it going longer. Brianna likes a game she and her Dad often play while she takes a bath. They take turns wrapping the soap up in the washcloth and pretending it is a present. Then they take turns giving it to each other, pretending it is a birthday present. They exclaim over what a lovely present

This play structure has an endless variety of uses. Children will never grow bored as they think up new ways to use it.

it is. This is a silly game, but the pleasure of playing it with Dad makes it special.

Selecting play materials

A major role of parents in play is to provide appropriate materials for play. Parents who want the best for their youngsters are concerned about providing educational experiences. This concern makes parents vulnerable to being misled by advertising claims. Most of the materials designed to *teach* are not worth the money. These materials tend to be limited to one type of use, involving a right or wrong way. Even if the challenge and skill level is a good match at first, those materials will soon grow boring. Additionally, they won't encourage creative thinking and problem solving if there is just one way to use them. Monique's friend Julia has some computer games that fit this description well. Julia's mom soon figured out that these so-called *games* were just glorified workbooks. Besides, Julia was frustrated with them and they weren't fun.

Toys that grow with a child, such as blocks, are the best investment. My son David built elaborate structures when he was 8 with the same blocks he started on when he was 3. Blocks are an example of materials that can be used however a child wishes, whatever ways create the appropriate challenge. Often this kind of play material is the box your new microwave oven came in, or the water in a puddle after a rain. Water play and sand play provide important learning opportunities to preschoolers. Materials for this type of play cost very little.

Inexpensive blank paper and markers encourage play with writing and can be used at any writing stage. Blank paper also encourages personally meaningful symbolic representation through drawing. It's too bad more parents aren't aware how much better blank paper is for their children than coloring books. With coloring books, children learn failure. Even after they have mastered *coloring in the lines*—a skill of dubious value, they still can't draw like the pictures in the books. Youngsters learn to consider the low-quality coloring-book pictures as standards for drawing; soon self-confidence as well as individual interpretation is lost. Adult models and expectations in any constructive play inhibits children's

Sand and water play provide important learning
opportunities to preschoolers.

development. Instead, children need to focus on
the process rather than the product; that is where
the value lies.

An environment for play

In addition to providing materials for play, you
can provide time and space for play. Children need
long periods of time to work through their ideas. If
you are aware of the importance of concentration

You probably have seen this type of symbolic representation—though you may not have liked it.

in play, you will minimize interruptions. You will postpone lunch until after the block tower is built, and you won't suggest a new activity while your child is engrossed in another one. Your respect for play will extend to providing a place for it. Blocks will be stored where there is an open space for building and where structures won't get knocked down by passersby.

When you value play, engage in it with your child and provide proper materials, adequate time and useful space, you are making major contributions to your child's education. Not only are these investments in your child's academic success, but these are investments in your child's emotional development and relationship with you.

A Guide to Playing With Your Child:
* Relax and enjoy the fun
* Forget about rules of games
* Let your child be in charge

How to Encourage Play:
* Pay attention to it
* Provide appropriate materials
* Provide space for it

Materials for Quality Play:
* Open-ended materials such as:
        Blocks, play dough
        Blank paper and markers
        Cardboard boxes
* Real materials such as sand and water
* Dress-up clothes

The training of preschool teachers and caregivers is even more important than the number of children per adult.

16

I Go to School

Brianna feels very big because she gets to go to *school,* while her baby sister only goes to the baby-sitter's house. Actually Brianna's school is called a *child-care center,* but differs from a preschool mainly in the number of hours it operates. The morning program at the child-care center is very similar to that of the cooperative preschool where Monique goes to school.

Group size

Each has a good ratio of adults to children, so there is always someone to help a child. The child-care center and the preschool each limit their number to no more than 20 children. Both offer age-appropriate activities under the direction of well-trained personnel. Research on child care has clearly proved that, with caregivers trained in child development, children in small groups develop higher levels of reading knowledge and verbal ability than those in larger groups.

For preschoolers, unlike younger children, the

total number of children in a program is more critical than how many adults per child there are. This may make a small family day-care home program an attractive alternative for some youngsters. Family home child-care programs run by trained and dedicated caregivers are a far cry from our old idea of a *baby-sitter.*

Teacher training

The training of preschool teachers and caregivers is of even greater importance than numbers of adults and children. Research cautions us that training should not be confused with years of experience. Apparently it is very possible to have been doing the wrong things with children for a long time. No one purposely provides inappropriate experiences for youngsters, they only do so out of ignorance. The current lack of standards for training in early childhood education results in many well-meaning—but uninformed—people teaching in counter-productive ways. Your job as a parent is to screen a preschool, child-care center or home program carefully before placing your child there.

A developmentally appropriate program

Programs designed to meet the needs of young children will help your child learn and grow in the same ways you are nurturing growth at home. Quality early-childhood programs will help your child become literate by using print in real-life and

You can tell that this preschool values block play—an important learning activity.

play activities. They will also allow him to explore freely with writing and will read to him frequently. Teachers who understand child development assist childrens' growth in literacy in ways similar to how they assist their language development. They encourage using both written and oral language in meaningful situations.

If you visit a preschool or child-care facility, take a good look around to see what the children are doing. Perhaps youngsters will be sitting at tables coloring commercially produced pictures or circling correct answers on worksheets. You'll know this program is not developmentally appropriate for your preschooler. It is one of many that simply borrowed activities designed for older children. They just watered them down for little kids. This approach reflects a common lack of understanding of the unique learning style of young children.

If children's art work all looks alike—or tries to—you'll know that teachers here are confused. They do not realize that the *process* and not the *product* is important for children's learning. Some adults make a model and try to teach young children how to copy it. They are depriving youngsters of the opportunity to freely explore with materials and discover their potential. Children need lots of opportunity to blob glue or paint on paper with no product at all in mind. Let them figure out what wonderful things they can do with these materials. The children are preoccupied with the process rather than the product. That's demonstrated by their usual lack of concern about the finished *masterpiece.*

Alex works at the easel in his child-care center, putting layer after layer of different colors on top of each other. The director, Janet, thought it was quite pretty before he proceeded to make everything a brown mess. But she focuses on what's important to him; the experience of painting. She doesn't ask preschoolers "What is it?" She knows that most preschoolers are not capable of realistic art work. Such a question suggests that realism is expected, making the child feel like a failure. After awhile, Alex wanders off to another activity. Although Janet carefully hangs his painting up to dry, Alex isn't interested in saving it or taking it home. The value of the painting was finished when he finished it.

Alex is free to move from one activity to

If children's art work all looks alike, you'll know the teacher is confused about how children learn.

another at will. This is a characteristic of good programs for preschoolers. It is important that they be able to choose what interests them from a wide variety of intriguing activities and materials. Janet and the teachers on her staff work very hard to maintain a stimulating learning environment. They

The teacher thought this picture was quite pretty at one time. But the child continued to add layer after layer of color. Knowledgeable teachers accept the process as more important than the product.

provide variety and novelty in activities. This way, children are surrounded with learning opportunities. They don't force any certain experiences at any time; they merely offer them. They don't expect, or want, all children to do the same things at the same time. When Janet asks for help in making the cornmeal muffins for snack, a few children are interested. Others are busy with many other exciting things. When just a few children are working with a teacher, the quality of interaction and language results in effective learning.

Play in preschool

Teachers who are qualified to assist young children's learning are skilled in facilitating play. Both Janet and Linda, Monique's teacher, value play and consider it the heart of their program. Linda's preschool has ideal space and can set aside large areas for different kinds of play. There is an indoor active play area with a climber, a balance beam and other equipment for large-muscle development. A block center is permanently available. It has room for props such as small cars, trucks, animals and people to use with the structures built there. The playhouse area is large, with space to hang dress-up clothes. There's a mirror to admire your costume, and storage for dishes and pots and pans. Sometimes water play moves into the playhouse to bathe dolls, wash dishes or to use for pretend cooking.

Some preschool teachers get upset if children take materials from one play area into another. Some schools have lots of rules about where kids can play with different equipment. But both Linda and Janet know that more sophisticated and valuable play occurs when different kinds of play materials are combined. A highly complex and motivating play situation was created in the pizza-parlor situation. The youngsters combined play-dough pizza, the playhouse oven, dress-up clothes for waiters, and paper and pencil for taking orders. You have seen how combining toy trucks or shovels in a sandbox keeps kids more involved. Children are interested in things that stimulate their

Shelves, unlike toy boxes, provide easy access to play
material.

minds. Single-use materials create sterile situations
that quickly become boring. Swing sets rusting in
so many yards are an example of single-use play-
things soon abandoned.

Part of valuing play is providing easy access to
play materials. Toy boxes are the worst-possible
way to store toys. Having toys in a toy box is like
having your kitchen utensils and food supplies all
thrown into one big box. You would have to pull
out everything each time you wanted to find anything. It would also be difficult to know exactly
what you have to work with. Janet and Linda keep
materials for children on low open shelves. Sets of
small items such as Leggos® or beads to string are
in small plastic containers on the shelves.

Some children choose to spend time in the cozy pillowed nook set aside for privacy.

Teacher role

Janet and Linda also spend time observing play. This not only demonstrates to children that their play is important, but it also gives the teachers much information about children's development. Both teachers make notes at the end of each day about new milestones in language or understanding made by different youngsters. They also make notes about behavior that concerns them and try to figure out how to help children who seem to be having a problem. In her all-day program Janet notices some children who need to have some time alone. Some children frequently choose to spend time in the cozy pillowed nook set aside for privacy.

Janet and Linda play with children, too. They are careful never to take charge and direct play, but

185

instead take their cues from the youngsters. Frequently Linda is invited into the playhouse for a cup of tea or to admire a baby's outfit. She makes the appropriate comments and asks questions which further the action. When children at Janet's center are fishing from the top of the climber with long strands of yarn, she asks about what kinds of fish they are catching. This encourages them to speculate about catching a shark or a whale—nothing as common as salmon or trout for them. Sometimes children profit from suggestions that help them elaborate their play.

The young preschoolers sometimes need help figuring out how to use some play materials. Alex was intrigued with the toy fire station and its many parts. Until Janet spent some time playing with these toys with him, he wasn't quite sure what to do with them. Older children in the center are also wonderful teachers of play. When 3-year-old Alex plays with 4-1/2-year-old Brianna, his play becomes much more complex. This is a benefit of multi-age grouping within programs. A day-care home with school-age youngsters returning in late afternoon offers another learning experience for younger children.

Literacy activities

Multi-age grouping is valuable at the writing center, just as in the playhouse or block center. As children discuss their writing, they learn much from one another. There is wide variety in the stages of writing in Janet's center, but all youngsters feel comfortable to write in their own way. Alex's writing scribbles are just beginning to look a little different from his drawing scribbles. Elise is making her scribbles in neat lines resembling writing. The older youngsters can make at least some of the letters in their own names and take pleasure in doing so. But writing isn't confined to the writing center. Janet leaves pad and pencil strategically beside the telephone in the playhouse, she places materials for making signs in the block center and has blank books included in the reading center in case someone is moved to write their own book. No wonder children in this center include writing in their play.

They also include reading in their play. Although there is a well-stocked book area featuring a changing array of good children's literature, there are books throughout the center. Reading happens everywhere. Books in the playhouse are for reading bedtime stories to babies or for being Mom or Dad relaxing. Books about guinea pigs are beside the guinea-pig cage. Books about seashells and marine life are included in the display of items children picked up on a trip to the beach this week. There are always some books in the privacy nook, too.

Reading and writing are a major part of life in both of these preschool programs. Neither teaches letters and sounds, but both help children use written language in purposeful ways. When children at Linda's school used a pasta-making machine, they followed a written recipe to make the dough. When they put away play materials, they see written

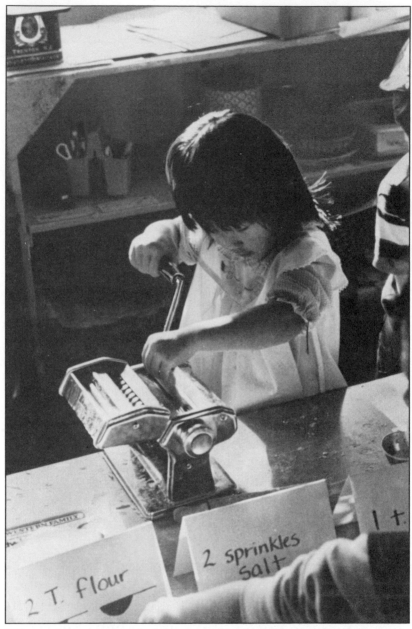

When the preschool class used a pasta maker, they followed written recipe cards. Reading and writing should be a major part of preschool, but not lessons on letters and sounds.

labels beside the pictures that remind them where things go. When children have something important to say, sometimes they ask for help in writing. There is someone available to write down whatever a child wants to dictate.

Brianna frequently asks for someone to write down information about dinosaurs as she dictates it. When her parents adopted her little sister, Janet helped Brianna record her feelings about that important event and make it into a book. Alex likes to tell his funny stories and have someone write them at school as well as at home. He is proud to point out his latest story displayed on the wall at school. Janet and Linda know that their students are making important progress in reading and writing through the activities in their programs. Both are skilled in assisting each child's growth at his or her own rate.

A good choice

When Carol came to pick up Alex after work today, she found him sitting on the floor and leaning against a teacher, engrossed in a story. There were just two other children listening to the same story, so each was having a quality experience. Each could see the picture and words in the book and each could exchange comments with the teacher about the story. Across the room Brianna was in another small group with a teacher who had agreed to read a dinosaur book Brianna had brought to school that day. The children seemed so contented and the scene was so peaceful that Carol was very reassured that she had chosen the right place for Alex to spend his time while she was at work.

Suppose you visit a preschool or preschool facility and find children involved in a variety of play activities. Perhaps you'll hear adults asking children about what they are doing instead of telling them what to do. If you see these things, you have probably found a developmentally appropriate program for your child. Do you also see children and adults using written as well as oral language in their work and play? If so, you have probably found a place that will nurture your child's emerging literacy. If this place also has enough loving adults so your child will be able to find a lap to sit on when needed, grab it.

When Choosing Preschool or Child Care, Look For:

* Enrollments of under 25 (15 best)
* A maximum of 10 children per teacher (5 best)
* Teachers or care-givers trained in early childhood education
* Lots of:

  Free choice
  Variety in activities
  Open-ended play
  Talking
  Uses of print
  Available play
    materials

  Space to play
  Teacher attention
  Books
  Writing materials
  Blocks
  Small, informal
    storytimes

* Some:

  Places for quiet and privacy
  Field trips and outings
  Cooking experiences
  Variation in ages

* Very little:

  Sitting and listening
  Teacher-directed instruction

* No:

  Workbooks or worksheets
  Letter and sound drill
  Handwriting lessons
  Look-alike art work

Section 5

Your Primary-grader Begins to Read & Write

Tanya watches her dad write and she wants to write, too.
Like all youngsters, she wants to imitate her dad.

17

A Writer in a Literate Society

Brandon watches with interest as his Dad makes out a list of things he needs to get for winterizing the boat. Pretty soon Brandon comes up to Jim with a paper on which he has written several letters, many upside-down and backwards. Brandon says, "Here Dad, these are the things you have to get." Jim accepts the paper with a thank you, and doesn't worry that his 5-year-old's *list* has mixed-up letters and no real words.

Mrs. Montoya, Brandon's kindergarten teacher, explained this to parents at the school Open House. Jim now knows children do a lot of exploring before they figure out how to write something so others can read it. Mrs. Montoya also explained the importance of children figuring out for themselves how to communicate with print. So Jim doesn't try to teach Brandon how to make his letters correctly or how to spell words correctly. Instead, he lets his son see him reading and writing and encourages Brandon's attempts at it.

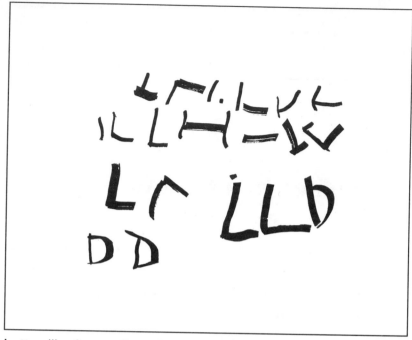

Letter-like forms: Brandon's list.

Uncritical role models

Brandon's admiration for his father makes him want to do the things he sees Jim doing, just as your child will want to imitate your activities. Your kindergartener may be at a level similar to Brandon's, or at a much different one. Mrs. Montoya told parents that her class of 5-year-olds includes children who are still scribbling and also some who can write full-page stories with readable spelling. This teacher accepts that each child progresses at an individual rate and that each comes to kindergarten with different levels of understanding. She tries to help parents accept these differences, too.

Some children seem hung up on writing their

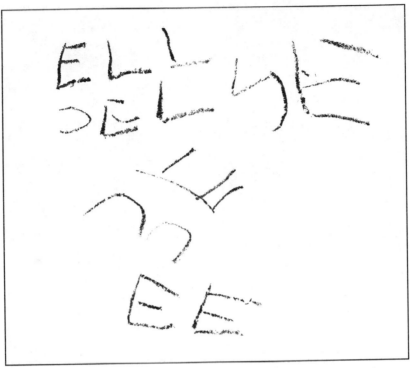

Elise's "writing." The letters of her name are the ones she uses for all writing.

names and will fill up a page with the letters of their name arranged in many different ways. Mrs. Montoya has just read research explaining this phenomenon. It demonstrates a child's discovery that written language uses a finite symbol system. This system reorganizes the same set of 26 letters to produce all words. A young child is apt to define the letters in his or her own name as *the* set of letters. Now, Mrs. Montoya can explain this stage of writing to parents.

She asks parents not to make a fuss about how letters are formed, just to encourage their children

Children feel that their writing is valued when they are given a blank "book" of stapled pages to write in. When they first realize there are certain letters for certain words, they may just write words they know. They need encouragement to work on new words.

to write. She also suggests encouraging youngsters to figure out how to spell words for themselves. Parents and caregivers should accept whatever the results are. At first Jim was worried about this, thinking Brandon would never learn the right way to spell or write. This is a common worry and one you are probably thinking about. Mrs. Montoya reassured Jim by comparing Brandon's method of learning about written language with how he learned about spoken language. Jim thought about how Brandon gradually changed his babbles and later baby talk to fairly grown-up speech. Then he realized that no one had to correct Brandon's mistakes for him. Jim was able to see for himself that children learn about both spoken and written language by constant exposure to them.

Invented spelling

By Christmas, Brandon has started to use certain letters for certain sounds when he writes. He has begun using *invented spelling*, figuring out for himself how words should be spelled. His letters are still backwards sometimes, but he notices his own errors more and more often. Jim encourages Brandon to write at home as well as at school. Some evenings Brandon works beside his Dad at the kitchen table while Jim does the paperwork for his fishing business. As a single parent, Jim doesn't have a lot of time to teach Brandon, but he can be sure his son sees him writing and he can react to Brandon's writing efforts with enthusiasm. When he has time, Jim asks Brandon to read what he has

> "WIN NOSGOL MIGRAIMM"
> Krista wrote this in Kindergarten and read it:
> "When there's no school my Grandma's gonna spend the night."

written. This gives Jim an idea of how fast his son is progressing. Jim is even starting to be able to read some of what Brandon writes. When he sees **yz** for the word *was,* he is glad that he learned from Mrs. Montoya about kids using letter names as sounds.

Supporting writing

Corey, another of Mrs. Montoya's students, is learning to write surrounded by a large family for inspiration. The activities of his two older brothers and his little sister are sometimes the topic of his writing. Sometimes he writes his feelings about his family. As a big brother, he wrote, "I wish I nuzzer (pronounced never) hadd a sister," and hastened to explain that he only felt that way sometimes. As a little brother he wrote, "I wish I wodd noover (another version of never) git pitun (picked on)." For Mother's Day he made a card that said, "Mom izz the grades (greatest)."

Everyone in Corey's family writes. His mom keeps writing materials on the kitchen counter where they are handy. She says they wouldn't be used so much if they were upstairs in the kids' bedrooms. Corey's little sister, Heidi, considers herself

Tanya wrote this in kindergarten: "I like to go swimming, especially on hot summer days."

Corey's pride in his emerging capabilities shows as he
writes: "I can ski; I can draw; I can read a book."

Figuring out how to symbolize an idea takes careful thought.

a writer, too, and proudly shows off the marks she makes on paper. Older brothers Todd and Chad have been taught to respect the writings of the younger children, so Corey confidently writes whatever he wants to. His pride in his emerging

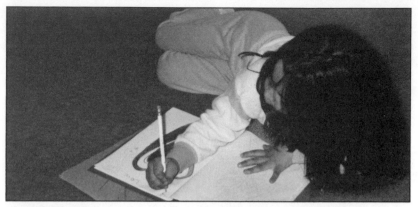

Children don't need to "learn their letters" before they can write. They learn about letters as they work at writing.

capabilities shows in some of the things he writes: "i can skcey, i can groo, i can reyd a book," boasts one page of writing. He doesn't worry about whether or not he can spell *ski, draw* or *read* correctly. As he reads this later, he points to *groo* and comments, "I forgot I was supposed to use a *d.*" He has made progress in the two weeks since he thought *draw* sounded like it started the same as *giraffe.*

Corey is an active little boy who fights monsters when he plays and when he writes. Before he wrote with letters, he told wonderful action-packed stories with pictures. Writing on the computer at school recently, he created a great version of *once upon a time*: "ousoopunootm ann thaer wooz a moonster and they rakt won hous." Sometimes he draws scary monsters and shows them saying things with the words in cartoon-style balloons.

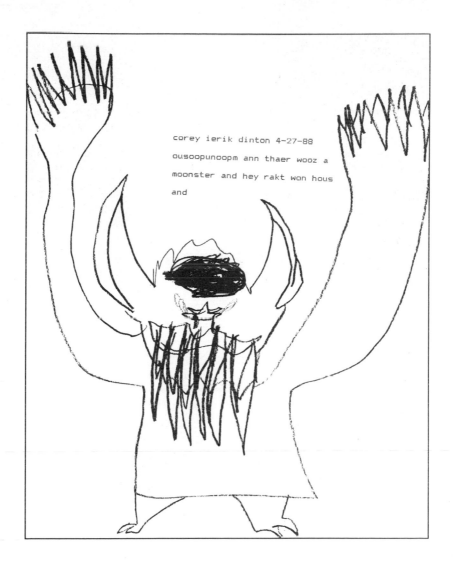

corey ierik dinton 4-27-88
ousoopunoopm ann thaer wooz a
moonster and hey rakt won hous
and

Learning to write by writing

Corey uses print for many purposes despite his lack of perfection with the form. We can learn from him that children don't need adults to correct their errors. We can also learn from Corey and other children that they don't need to *know their letters* before they can write. It is through writing that they

Jan. 3, 1987

Today we went to the beach!
I went snorkeling in the shalow-
end for practes.
It is 5:00. In about 5 miqutes
I well go back to the beach.
I saw clear fish in the water.
And about 5 school's of fish.

Near-standard spelling is readable.

learn their letters, not the other way around.
Corey's mom says Corey is making much faster progress than his older brothers who received traditional instruction in letters, sounds and spelling
when they started school.

Summer's parents, Tom and Sue, encourage
her writing also. She is in second grade and gaining competence rapidly. She has had teachers who
help children learn phonics principles through
reading and writing experiences. She hasn't been
taught by isolated drill with workbooks or flash-
cards. Her second-grade teacher still encourages
invented spelling. Summer hasn't had to deal with
adults telling her dozens of phonics rules that don't
make sense and are hard to remember, and she
hasn't had to face intimidating spelling lists. She is
confident of her ability to write because of the confidence adults have in her; she is eager to write because she hasn't been criticized for her immature
penmanship and spelling. Consequently, she
doesn't limit her writing to words she knows how
to spell. She writes complex compositions with
words such as *tranch ala* and *acshily.*

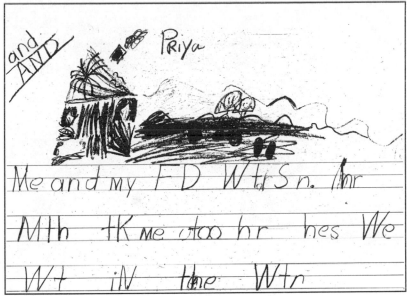

Invented spelling: "Me and my friend went swimming. Her mother took me to her house. I went in the water."

Spelling progress

Last year Summer's spelling was so far from standard that her parents usually needed to have her read her writing to them. They did learn some of her spelling strategies, though. Tom noticed that her beginning spelling simplified words to the basics. It was rather like her beginning speech when she was younger. In each case, just the most obvious sounds were included. So **hs** spelled *house* and **sn** spelled *swimming*. Gradually Summer was able to add more and more sounds; but Tom really had to work to figure out what *blobre peken* said. Sue had been with Summer on her outing, so she knew it spelled *blueberry picking."*

The more Summer wrote, the more wonderful

As children gain maturity and confidence, they notice more and more about the way words are spelled and sentences punctuated.

her writing became and the more normal her spelling looked. She recently wrote a seven-page letter that was perfectly readable. And she kept a journal during a family trip. Her mom says, "Letting them write in their own way is really the way to do it. Now, Summer gets nothing but 100s on her spelling tests; just a little while ago I couldn't even translate her writing."

It's a lot easier for kids as well as adults to write with a word processor.

Tom and Sue do a lot of writing in their work. Tom also writes songs as part of his avocation as a musician. They could understand when Summer's teacher explained that spelling, punctuation and other polishing are best left until the final draft. Sue has discovered this principle for herself in writing with a computer, which allows her to go back later and easily make corrections. She can write more fluently when she doesn't have to worry about editing details as she goes. She encourages her

tania 5-24-88

i wel i wod l i ctogoi gin l gaghepwef m

mom

Written in kindergarten by Tania who read it: "I would like to go on a trip with my Mom."

daughter to do the same whether with a computer or by hand. As a beginner, it is important for Summer to gain confidence and fluency in writing before she concerns herself with perfection.

As Summer gains maturity and experience, she will notice more and more about the way words are spelled and sentences are punctuated. Her writing gives her experience to become a better reader. Her reading provides models to help her become a better writer. She will soon have sufficient knowledge and skill to make her spelling and punctuation more like she sees it in books. Meanwhile, her parents still see some very strange spellings: *naew* for *now* as Summer overdoes the sounding-out process. For awhile she put a silent **e** on the end of

A GIRL LOVES A BOY
Once opon a time girl livd.
Her name was Dorlen.
She had a boyfrnd.
She loved im so much she
evne kisst him.
One day she kisst him 12 timse

all words whether they needed it or not. She also went through a period of sprinkling silent **gh** and silent **K** randomly in words. It's all part of the process of children trying to make sense of our complex sound-symbol system.

Appropriate feedback

When Summer desires to perfect a piece of writing, then feedback on spelling and punctuation are appropriate and helpful. You, like Summer's parents, will want to exercise caution as an editor. If you try to correct everything at once, your child will become discouraged. Take it slow and focus on a few things at a time. Go ahead and provide the accepted spelling of all the words, if your child wants you to. But it is better to concentrate on a few frequently used words each time. Punctuation rules should be doled out *slowly*. If you aren't sure how far to go, ask your child's teacher which punctuation is being covered at school. Tanya's teacher is now recommending only the most basic concept: put spaces between words.

Just as Sue and Tom don't polish everything they write, they don't expect Summer to perfect everything she writes, either. Some things are just for personal use or for playing around. First drafts are to focus on ideas instead of writing mechanics. Only things you write formally for someone else's benefit need to be edited. This attitude keeps Summer writing because the fun is emphasized and the drudgery is downplayed. Summer writes poetry, songs and fantasy as well as accounts of her actual adventures and letters to relatives. Summer, Brandon and Corey are all on their way to becoming life-long writers, truly literate people.

**Encouraging your
Primary-grade Child to Write**

* Accept your child's level of understanding
* Be sure your child sees you writing
* Relax about spelling and handwriting
* Learn to read and enjoy invented spelling
* Keep writing materials handy
* Remember the role of reading in learning to write
* Give criticism only when asked, and then sparingly

18

You Read & Then I Read

Corey's mother just discovered that he could read. He told her he wanted to read for her, so Sharon helped him find one of the easier books in the bookshelf. Sure enough, he could read. Now Corey plans to take a book to school and surprise his teacher by reading to her. Neither his mother nor teacher has specifically instructed him in reading, but both supported his efforts to become literate.

How Corey learned to read

When asked how he learned to read, Corey said, "I just tried and I did it. Without any help." He thinks a little more and adds, "Maybe I learned most words from writing—like this word and this word." He points to words in the book as he talks. Corey's hypothesis about how he learned to read is supported by researchers studying beginning reading. Indeed children do learn to read by writing, and they do it themselves. These new research findings contradict traditional assumptions about

Corey surprises his teacher by showing her he has discovered how to read.

how children learn to read. This guides us into different ways of assisting beginning readers.

"Some of these sort of don't make sense," apologizes Corey as he reads a Dr. Seuss beginning-reader book. Corey understands the purpose of print and is aware that this book sacrifices meaning to achieve a simple vocabulary. However, he tries to give it meaning by reading with expression. When he gets stuck on a word, his mom doesn't tell him to "sound it out." Instead of focusing on the sounds of letters, she helps him focus on the meaning by asking, "What do you think would make sense?" This question helps Corey figure out that he should read *how* rather than *now*. He comments, "How, by, you—I get some of those words mixed up." Abstract words such as these are commonly the ones that give youngsters the most trouble because they have no meaning in themselves. Corey has no trouble reading the words *Marvin K. Mooney* though, because these words refer to a person in the story.

Picture clues help Corey, as they do most beginning readers. He corrected himself when he noticed that the picture he saw didn't correspond to the word he read. Books with pictures to help tell the story are important for youngsters who are just beginning to read. However, if it is just the picture that tells the story, there is no reason to read. Corey comments on that issue as he reads another book, "The problem is it gives you a clue on most pages." This book actually required no reading; mastering the repetitious pattern and reading pictures was all that was required. This would be appropriate for a child at an earlier stage, but Corey was ready for more challenge.

Corey does pay close attention to the print as well as the pictures when he reads. Once he inserted an additional word in a sentence as he read but noticed that it didn't fit. What he had done was change the wording to match his own speaking style. This is frequently done by readers who are reading for meaning rather than saying words.

Neither Sharon nor Mrs. Montoya would have corrected him on this error. A slight change in wording that doesn't affect the meaning is actually a sign of good reading. It's really not an error. Corey's mom responds to beginning reading errors the same way she responds to beginning writing and talking errors. There's acceptance and pleasure for whatever level a child demonstrates.

Maturation and reading

Most children can't just pick up a book and read it by the end of kindergarten. Corey's parents gave him an advantage by starting him in kindergarten when he was 6 instead of 5. Corey's Mom used to be a teacher. She knew some kids who were barely old enough to start school had a hard time. Considering his size and maturity, Corey seemed like one of those kids to her. Besides, his brothers were old for their grades and starting Corey later kept things even. So Corey got an extra year of preschool and turned into an *early* reader instead of a *late* one. Maturation is a big factor in children's learning. No amount of pushing can alter the rate of maturation. Corey's mom and dad, Sharon and Bruce, don't want their kids to feel pressured or pushed at all. They're pleased with their decision to hold Corey back.

Creating eager readers

Sharon's way of helping her children become readers is not to conduct lessons in reading, but to

Reading along with a tape-recorded story is a big help in learning to read. A puppet can help, too.

share her own joy in reading. With her first child, she did some directed-instruction activities. Since then, she's learned new and more effective approaches. Even though both she and Bruce work, they usually find time to take their family to the library twice a week. Each child has his or her own library card and everyone, including Bruce and Sharon, checks out books.

Corey certainly loves books. When asked about his favorites, he replies, "I'll tell you my best book—EVERY ONE!" He qualifies that statement with, "I like all the books, but I don't really like chapter books." Corey is aware that, like most youngsters his age, he is not ready for novels yet. He's familiar with books appropriate to his age. This shows in his ability to discuss books by authors as well as titles.

He has favorite authors and can tell you what books they wrote. He likes Shirley Hughes' books such as *George the Babysitter* and *Alfie*. Martha Alexander wrote *Nobody Asked Me If I Wanted a Baby Sister*, and other books that make Corey laugh. He loves the excitement of Steven Kellogg's *Island of the Skogg* and the fantasy tales Tomie de Paola illustrates so beautifully. He also mentions a children's author he knows personally, Jean Rogers who wrote *King Island Christmas*. Some Dr. Seuss books he enjoys are *McElligott's Pool* and *To Think I Saw It On Mulberry Street*. These are all books his parents read to their kids. The family also has a collection of the beginning-reader books such as the *Dr. Seuss Beginners* book he first read to Sharon.

Corey's parents read to their children frequently, whenever they can fit it into their busy schedule of Little League, Cub Scouts, piano lessons, school and their own jobs. With several children, there is always lots going on. But when the family is together in the evening, they read. Television is not the center of their living room. In fact they only have a small black-and-white set that gets just one local channel. Sharon and Bruce read for their own purposes as well as reading to their children. This is the model their children follow.

Children figure out phonics principles in the process of picking out which word is which.

Self-directed lessons

When Sharon or Bruce read to Corey, he wants to see the page. He often asks questions such as "Where are you right now? Are you reading that word?" He is working at figuring out more and more about written language. If children look at the print while you read to them, they learn a great deal about letters and sounds. This is especially true of stories they have heard over and over until they memorize them. They begin to try and pick out which word is which. They figure out many phonics principles in the process. Through these kinds of experiences, Corey is rapidly gaining in his ability to read independently. But he still needs quite a bit of assistance reading most books. He likes to try a little, then turn it back to Mom or Dad. "First you read and then I'll read," seems like a good compromise.

His school friend Tanya is also in the process of learning to read. Although she is in his class, she is a full year younger than Corey. She is at a different stage in her reading development. Although she isn't reading in the traditional sense, she can *read* a wordless picture book with great expression and colorful language. As she prepares to read Spiers' *Noah's Ark,* she explains, "This doesn't have any words so you get to make up your own story." When she encounters some unexpected writing on one page, she deals with it decisively: "You pretend there are no words when there are some."

She shows her knowledge of books as she carefully reads the title on the cover from memory. Then she turns each page carefully, telling the story seriously and with formal language appropriate to the story: "The birds were singing with joy." The rich detail of the pictures is reflected in her narrative. One picture of a mouse trying to shove an elephant's foot off another mouse's tail prompts her to read, "'Yeow!' said the mouse, 'get off my

Books with pictures to help tell the story are important for youngsters who are just beginning to read.

friend's tail.'" She shows a fine understanding of dialogue in text.

Tanya's interpretations are sometimes unique, as when she describes the olive branch the dove brings back to the ark at the end of the flood. Tanya decides it is food, but can tell from the pictures that it is well-received. She reads, "The animals were DELIGHTED!" Then as the pictures reveal Noah showing the branch to each animal, she continues, "Every kind of animal licked it." And finally finished, "The cow ate it."

For awhile, a child may be too pleased with her new reading skills to let anyone else read to her.

She uses her previous knowledge to bring meaning to this book. She can identify almost all the animals, even the snails in a jar. She also uses her background information when she reads, "The water got deep. It was flooding outside." She is able to explain at this point, "I think Jesus did it." After a minute she modifies that statement, "Actually God did it."

Enjoying books

After she finishes reading, she is ready for an adult to read to her. Her pleasure in reading and books is evident as she shows me the book she wants me to read to her. "You're going to love this! This is the funniest," she assures me. This child is capable of gaining much pleasure and information from books. This is true even though she isn't yet able to decode written language. She also knows a great deal about literary style and language. She is definitely learning to read.

Summer is too pleased with her new reading skills to want someone else to read to her, unless it is her grandfather. Instead of having her parents read to her, now she wants to read to them. And she does so with great expression, demonstrating her understanding and joy in what she reads. She notices that some other kids read in a monotone and asks her mom why they read like that.

She can read most any book she chooses. This week when she went to the library, she chose one of Bill Peet's books, *Encore for Eleanor,* and *Space Witch,* another book by the author of *Corduroy* which she liked when she was younger. Summer is also getting interested in the books her older sister is reading, the Beverly Clearly books such as *Ramona and Her Father,* and books by Judy Blume like *Are You There God? It's Me, Margaret.* A great favorite of both girls is *Bet You Can't: Science Impossibilities to Fool You.* Summer and her sister read nonfiction as well as fiction, and the stack of books by each of their beds testifies to the fact that they both read a lot.

Corey, who is almost 7, and Tanya, who is barely 6, are both beginning readers at their own stage. Both are making good progress in becoming literate, nurtured by constant exposure to good books. Summer will have her eighth birthday soon and has already taken off in reading.

Supporting Your Beginning Reader

DO

* Keep reading times relaxed and enjoyable
* Accept your child's own rate of maturation
* Continue to read to and with your child
* Help your child find books of personal interest
* Ask, "what would make sense?" when child is stuck on a word

DON'T

* Say, "sound it out" when child is stuck on a word
* Worry about errors that don't change meaning
* Use books with pictures that tell the whole story

19

Learning by Doing

Young children learn by doing. Activity is the key to quality early-childhood education. Children learn important concepts through experiences with objects and events in their world. And they learn about reading and writing through experiences with written language in their world. Young children learn from experiences where they get to do something, touch things and find out what happens. This is *active* learning, as opposed to the *passive* approach of sitting and listening to others tell you what they have learned.

Active learning

Television and computer games also offer the opposite of active learning. Computer-software advertisements talk about interactive learning. When you try out the program, you will see that kids' action is generally confined to pressing the right button. With very few exceptions, the computer has the answers; the child is not encouraged to think of new ones. Those few games that allow

Tanya has her own rake for helping with yard work. In the process she is learning a great deal about how things grow.

children some control over what happens on the screen, although of limited value, are the best choice. No matter what software you use, the computer is limited to showing pictures and symbols; a child can't have real experiences with objects on a screen.

Your primary-grade child still has much in common with younger children in the need to learn through the senses. Primary children are more sophisticated than toddlers in how they explore, being less likely to put strange things into their mouths. Nevertheless, young school-age children require the opportunity to touch and examine their environment firsthand. Pictures and films are a nice accompaniment to firsthand experiences, but not a substitute for them.

Family-style learning

Tanya's family life provides a wide variety of experiences: they go boating, swim frequently, take family trips and garden. There is also much about nature for Tanya to explore in her own yard. She has grown up with two dogs for playmates. The addition of a baby sister to the family adds further to Tanya's repertoire of experiences. She is able to bring a good understanding to her reading as a result of her background.

Out in the yard, she turns over a piece of log and exclaims, "Yuk!" She points with fascination at the slug she has uncovered. Then she discovers some dead bugs in a pool of rainwater, simultaneously expressing revulsion and demonstrating her interest. These experiences add interest and meaning to her many nonfiction books that discuss the why's and how's of nature. As she looks at a book on insects, she comments, "I like spiders because they eat bumble bees and things. I saw one eat a bug once."

Tanya likes to help her folks in the yard. She has her own small rake and shovel to make her work easier. Watching the strawberries coming up is an exciting reward. In the process, she is learning a great deal about how things grow. She has learned much about water and tides as part of boating trips. Wearing a small replica of Dad's wool fishing jacket, she carries life preservers and boat cushions down to the boat. They had to check the tidebook carefully to determine when the tide would be right for getting in and out of their cove.

Although Tanya can't explain the scientific facts behind tide changes, she has an excellent practical understanding of this phenomenon.

Gaining understanding

No amount of explanation, oral or written, could possibly give Tanya the level of understanding about scientific facts that her real-life experiences provide. She is gaining in her knowledge of the world and in her ability to think and analyze. Chris and Gail, her dad and mom, help her get the most from these experiences. They know that she learns more by trying to figure things out for herself than if they give her answers. So they ask questions about what she thinks rather than giving her information. If some of her hypotheses are far-out, they generally don't correct her. They know she has lots of exploring to do and plenty of time to do it before she is grown-up.

Because he lives in Alaska, Corey has some unique experiences. He takes for granted the Great Blue Heron that spends summers near a pond in his yard. "He goes to Seattle when it gets Christmas," he explains. Corey's vision of Seattle as *going South* and his equation of winter with Christmas may not be entirely accurate, but he is using his personal experiences to make sense of what he sees and hears. This is much more meaningful than merely memorizing someone else's explanation. As he gets older and is better able to understand abstract concepts, his understanding will become more sophisticated.

Corey has lots to say about participating in a bikeathon
with his family.

It doesn't take something unique to be special to a youngster. Corey has lots to say about participating in a bikeathon with his family. They were riding their bikes 26 miles as part of a fundraiser for the Diabetes Association. This was especially important to Corey's family because a friend had just been diagnosed as having diabetes. But what Corey wants to talk about is his adventure of having a flat tire during the bikeathon, "My tire poofed down and I only got to go seven miles." He describes in graphic detail the sounds of his tire popping and explains that he rode the rest of the way on the back of his Dad's bike. In this experience, he has learned quite a bit about how far 26 miles is compared to seven miles, he has learned something about the inside of a tire and he has learned that his parents think helping others is important. All of these understandings will enrich both his reading and his writing.

Importance of play

Play continues to be an important learning experience for school-age children. They still need the dramatic play, constructive play and large-muscle play described for preschoolers. Tanya's Dad designed a fantastic outdoor play structure. It offers a seemingly endless variety of options for use. You can climb up it on a rope net or on a sloping wall of slats, or on more challenging footholds. You can even try to shinny up the metal pole. Kids love to slide down the pole even if they can't come up that way. A slide offers another way down. The areas up on top suggest ideas for dramatic play. Sometimes there are pirates up there, or super-heroes and even astronauts. A nearby sandpile is available for the constructive play of making things out of sand. The availability of water to add to the sand helps keep this play interesting. Tanya's friends enjoy coming to play because her yard offers materials for challenging complex play.

School-age children benefit from play in the same ways preschoolers do. Play expands their ability to concentrate and enlarges their vocabu-lary. It also enhances their knowledge base and provides for their emotional needs. Primary-grade children still aren't ready for games with rules or winners and losers. They still profit most from the free exploration of open-ended play. These chil-dren will use writing in their play more often than younger ones. Older children will more often make signs to identify their block or sand structures such as, "ARPT Wr THE ArPLANS LNDE" (Airport where the airplanes land.) They are also more likely to create props with print.

Play and language development

Summer writes out tickets for the plays or musi-cal performances she and her sister put on for their parents. Her dramatic play has been influenced by the professional dramatic and musical productions she has attended with her parents. She draws the content of her plays from her real-life knowledge base, and creates the form based on her observa-tions at the theater. This is a way of pulling togeth-

Corey shows a sophisticated language ability as he puts on a puppet show with stuffed animals.

er her experiences and expressing them creatively. Whether she writes a script or keeps it in her head, she is gaining valuable practice with language skills.

Corey likes to put on puppet shows. I saw him use stuffed animals for puppets and the back of a couch for a puppet stage. He hid behind the couch, making up dialogue for the puppets as he pranced them around on top of the couch back. He changed his voice for the different characters, growling for the stuffed bear, "You can never get away from me!" He used words not part of his everyday vocabulary as the ape replied, "You are in my domain." He also played the role of narrator with transitional statements such as: "A little while later." In addition, he was the sound effects person, making slapping sounds on the wall during a fight, barking like a dog, and crying for a hurt character. His 3-year-old sister was entranced. She whispered, "It's funny," and laughed frequently. She got upset at the villian, responding like the audience in old-fashioned melodramas.

When you observe sophisticated uses of language like these, it is hard to remember how recently a child learned to talk. These children, like yours, learned an incredible amount about how to use oral language without formal instruction in the structure of the English language. They experienced language constantly from birth and gradually figured out how to use it for all kinds of purposes. They are learning to use written language in just the same way.

Surrounded by reading

Corey talks about the sign being off the boys' and girls' bathrooms at school for awhile and the resulting confusion. He can easily read those signs now that they have been replaced. This is meaningful print in a recognizable context. He might not recognize the word *boys* in a book, but he can recognize it on the door to the bathroom. Contex-

Corey can read his classmate's names on school charts.
This classroom is filled with print in contexts he can read.

tualized print experiences continue to provide important reading practice for youngsters after they start school.

Corey's and Tanya's classroom is filled with print in contexts they can read. They have learned to read most of their classmate's names from using them for the attendance chart and the jobs chart. In addition, they frequently check names on the birthday display. Recently, a chart showing each child's name and phone number was put up. Because they enjoy reading each other's names, Mrs. Montoya has created a bingo game with name strips instead of cards. They match randomly drawn letters of the alphabet to the letters in their friends' names. This is much better practice in recognizing letters than worksheets where children circle isolated letters out of context.

One bulletin board in the class shows photo-graphs of their pets. Under each photo is a caption such as, "Tanya's dogs." Children can read these captions and the ones under their string-painting pictures, too. Each child created an abstract design with string, paint and a folded paper; then each decided what the design reminded them of. Mrs. Montoya wrote for them as they told her their picture looked like ostriches, whales, muscle men and many more. The children enjoy reading the titles and trying to see that same thing in the pictures.

Much of the writing in the classroom has been dictated by the children. There is a chart telling about their trip to the beach, a giant ice-cream cone with favorite flavors written on it and a story about making juice. Children do a lot of dictation even though they are also trying to write independently. Your child will still benefit from dictating stories and ideas for you to write at home, too. It is a lot of work to write when you are just learning how. Sometimes a secretary makes it a lot easier to get good ideas down on paper.

At home, Corey finds things to read posted on the refrigerator—the family message center. He can point out on the school calendar which days he has gym and proudly reads that word. Use of print in his family has been an important part of his emerging literacy. He sees his parents and his older brothers finding out about a lot of things by reading notices and signs. He doesn't want to be left out and is fast figuring out how to decipher the print he encounters.

Summer writes notes frequently, using print to

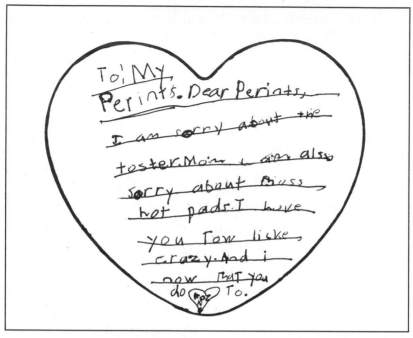

The child who wrote this note has a clear understanding of the power of print. She can use writings for important purposes even though she hasn't quite mastered spelling and punctuation.

make personal contact. Her understanding of written language as a substitute for oral language is shown in a note that begins, "Dear Dad, This is your daughter speaking." Her understanding of written language as a way of communicating with a person who is not there is also clear. She creates a constant flow of notes to her father when he is away on business. Tom has also been greeted with welcome home notes such as, "I aem so glad that you aer bak P.S. Dad I hav a sapris." When Summer wrote a note to the tooth fairy, she received an elaborate reply written in exotic-looking script.

Her dad went to a lot of trouble to encourage her joy in writing.

When your child sees you use written language to gain information and to communicate to others, you are helping your child learn to read and write. When you help your child figure out the meaning of print in the environment (not just the sounds), you are teaching a reading lesson. When you encourage your child to explore with writing, you are providing writing instruction. Remember, children learn much more from the real uses of reading and writing than from workbooks and readers.

Experiences To Support
Literacy Growth for 5- to 7-year-olds

* Biking
* Boating
* Climbing
* Fishing
* Gardening
* Play acting
* Pretend play
* Swimming
* Swinging
* Sand-pile play
* Traveling
* Caring for baby sister
* Caring for family pet
* Using print in play
* Using written signs and notices
* Seeing their thoughts in print
* Sending and receiving notes
* Seeing adults using print
* Seeing adults reading

20

Choosing the Very Best

Children's early-school experiences form attitudes that tend to persist throughout their school careers. They decide whether or not school is interesting. And, they decide whether they are smart. Children whose early experiences lead them to negative conclusions on either of these points are less likely to put energy into school. As a parent, you must know this. That's why you are so concerned that your child's teachers will make learning exciting and help your child feel successful.

Parents want the best school experiences and the "best" teachers for their children. Unfortunately, most parents don't know how to recognize what is best. Having read about how your child learns at this age, you are now better equipped to judge whether or not a given teacher will be a good match. You have the right to express a teacher preference and the right to observe teachers before choosing. When you observe a classroom, you will be looking for active learning and an atmosphere that accepts young children at their own level.

Corey's teacher has encouraged him to build on what he already knows. This is a picture-story of the eruption of a volcano that Corey shows off with pride.

New research

Recent research has radically altered traditional assumptions about good educational practices, especially in the area of reading. We now know that the best school experience for our children is not the same type of experience we had. When we were young, most of us dutifully went through our phonics lessons, did our workbook pages and pretended to follow along at reading time. We probably weren't clear about why we had to do all those things, but still tried to please our teachers. Then, during our free time, we played at writing and tried to read some interesting stories. Pretty soon we could read and we could write— and our teachers got the credit!

Studies of how children actually learn demonstrate that they often learn in spite of how they are taught rather than because of it. We now know that traditional education practices often hindered actual learning. These took up valuable time with meaningless drills. Traditional-education practices also quickly made some children feel like failures as early as first grade. You were probably aware of this, even as a child.

Choosing a teacher

You should look for a teacher who will help your child feel capable, smart and confident as a learner. That teacher will be skilled at building on what children already know and assisting them to discover more. That teacher will nurture your child's growth at school in much the same way you nurture that growth at home. What is good educational practice at home is also good educational practice in school. Teachers who have specific backgrounds in early-childhood education know how young children learn and how to assist that learning most effectively.

Corey's mother is pleased with the education he is receiving compared to the more traditional approaches his older brothers experienced. She says that Corey is much more excited about school and is progressing faster than his brothers. The big difference is in Corey's fluency as a writer. He has been free from worries about whether words were spelled right or letters formed correctly. Instead of drill on letters and sounds, Corey has been encouraged to write at school. Mrs. Montoya accepted pictures in his writing journal and strings of letters in his computer writing for a long time. She had faith that he would start putting sounds and symbols together as soon as he was ready. It took quite a while for him to get started. But once he did, Corey's progress has been amazing. He made the breakthrough on his own. He really understood how writing worked because he figured it out through his own exploration. With this solid understanding, he will continue to grow rapidly as a writer and as a reader.

Corey's parents will want him to have a first-grade teacher with the same approach to reading and writing that his kindergarten teacher had. They want him to continue writing freely without having someone telling him all the mistakes he has made. This requires a teacher who understands that children learn the mechanics of written language because they are writers and readers, not a teacher who still thinks that you learn to read and write by learning the rules. The teacher Corey's parents are looking for has faith in children's ability to correct their own early misspellings. She will compare this to how they corrected their own baby talk, without someone pointing out their errors. This teacher will see writing as a natural process learned much the same way as oral language.

In searching for the best classroom for Corey, Sharon will not only look for free exploration with writing, she will also look for free choices in reading. She wants Corey to stay excited about reading and knows that reading required stories in the reading book is not necessarily going to interest him. She believes Corey will learn to read better with material selected by topic rather than by vocabulary level. The *controlled vocabulary* of reading textbooks makes it hard for them to be interesting. These textbooks are created with the old idea that kids learn to read from recognizing words. Research now shows the reverse:

Kids learn to recognize words from reading.

Still little kids

The first-grade classroom Sharon wants for Corey will not be much different from his kindergarten classroom. Sharon knows Corey will still be pretty much the same kid next year that he was this year: active, talkative and curious. She wants a teacher who expects first graders to be just a tiny bit older than kindergarteners, not totally transformed. This teacher will have to understand the importance of play in young children's learning. She'll provide plenty of time and materials for play. Sharon knows that blocks, a playhouse, a water table, paint easels and manipulative materials such as Bristle Blocks® and Leggos® belong in a first grade just as much as in kindergarten. She wants Corey to be free to move around, talk and explore in first grade just as much as in kindergarten.

If Sharon visits a classroom where all of the children are sitting quietly at their desks for a long time, she will look elsewhere. She is especially concerned about teachers who keep children quiet at this age. They are still in their language-acquisition stage and need to practice their new language skills. Even second-grade classrooms should not be still and quiet places. Summer thrives in her classroom, where student interaction is not just allowed, but encouraged.

A first-grade classroom should not be radically different from a kindergarten. First graders are only a little older than kindergarteners.

A writing process

Summer's teacher has learned about the new way of teaching writing; hers is not a quiet classroom. This approach teaches youngsters the technique professional writers use. It shows them the steps to a quality finished product. The first step is talking about books, experiences or ideas that interest them as they search for topics of interest. Then each child works on a rough draft using his or her own topic. No more "everybody write about their pets," whether you have any or not. After that children share what they have written, reading it to a few friends and getting feedback.

Summer's teacher taught her students how to give each other constructive feedback. The emphasis at this point is on whether or not the meaning is clear and the content is interesting. The next stage is to rewrite, working on meaning and style. Children may or may not want to seek peer feedback again. The final stage involves editing for spelling, punctuation, grammar and other mechanics. Up until this point no such corrections have been made. Just as with professional writers, editing for young writers occurs at the final-draft stage. Here the teacher assists with correction of errors and uses the child's own writing to teach mechanics. Only on the final finished copy do children have to worry about penmanship for handwritten work or format in computer-typed work. This frees them during the composition phase to concentrate on getting their message across. What an improvement from children we

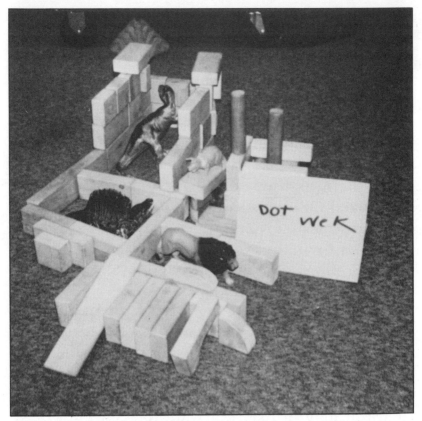

Play can incorporate print in a variety of ways. This sign demonstrates children's knowledge of the power of print.

have seen who limited their writing to things they could spell.

Although the emphasis is not on the mechanics of writing, children better learn mechanices through this approach, also. Teachers all over the country are reporting that their students are doing better on standardized spelling tests without having had the weekly spelling lists. More

Translation	lynda5-16-88
One upon a time there lived (a) ittle girl. Her name (was)	wispintime thr lvdilgrll hrnamoi
Becky . they fish and caught too many fish.	beke thwfish and kit tomanefish
It filled up the boat	it fild up the bot
But I did not care	but i did not kar
We finally gotted finally got home . . .	wai fale gatid filnle git hom hte
With fish and we ate the fish then	witfish and sasiat th fish th
Went for (ride or walk) we . . .	witfo ritk wai sacas paseba waga
said hello when got home we ate the fish	sadhl hello wanitom wia atth fish
then we went to bed . . .	th wia eiatobed thtalat
The next morning went to McDonald's	th nas moarn wito makdal
Ate fish sandwich	atfishsawh
That was yum.	that was jum
The next morning we took a nap in a	th na smoni eia tokanap inani
We had jello for lunch.	wihad jello folah

Children become fluent writers when they are freed from premature pressure to spell correctly.

important, children are demonstrating their spelling knowledge in their writing. With the old approach, teachers complained that there was no carryover from the spelling lists to actual writing. Children would misspell words when they wrote that they spelled correctly on the weekly test. It is evident that children learn a wide variety of things best through actual experience rather than rote memorization.

How young children learn

Active learning through play and free exploration characterizes quality early-childhood education from preschool through the primary grades. The differences between programs for children of different ages should be in the level of sophistication the children demonstrate. All early-childhood environments should provide a variety of new and interesting things to investigate, freedom for children to explore in their own ways and a teacher who can help children extend their understanding and knowledge. Young children thrive best with a teacher who is a guide and facilitator rather than a dispenser of knowledge. This type of teacher knows how to ask the right question at the right time. This teacher is ready with more materials to help children explore an idea further for themselves. And this teacher encourages "looking it up" when kids want information.

Teachers of young children must be experts on a lot of things. Look for someone who has a background in early-childhood education for an understanding of how young children learn best. Then look for someone who understands the Whole Language philosophy of reading and writing described in this book. This is the combination that will best help your child to become literate, as well as to enjoy school and learning.

Good Schools for 5-, 6- and 7-year-olds

* Understand the unique learning style of young children
* Help children learn from their own exploration and discovery
* Help children feel confident and successful
* Emphasize progress rather than mistakes
* Allow for different rates of learning and different levels of maturation
* Teach to children's interests
* Encourage learning through play
* Encourage active learning
* Encourage talking in school

Good Reading Programs for 5-, 6- and 7-year-olds

* Have no isolated drill on phonics or vocabulary
* Teach phonics through reading and writing
* Teach spelling through reading and writing
* Teach punctuation through reading and writing
* Allow children to choose their reading material
* Show children how to read for pleasure and information
* Encourage children to write for a variety of personal purposes

If your child is having problems at school, comfort and support is needed.

21

Trouble-shooting

What if you can't find a teacher who understands how young children learn? What if you get one who gives your child a daily dose of low self-esteem? Or what if your child is failing in school? And what if your child has a problem with learning? These are all serious concerns that parents frequently face.

Parents have the final say

No matter which of these problems you are facing, you have the ultimate say in your child's education. Don't let anyone convince you otherwise. You can make things better for your child. Marie has taken on the school system in defense of her son, Zach. She says, "I'm not willing to be sweet at the expense of my children." She thinks too many parents are intimidated by the schools.

"I won't let people who have known him for only a couple months tell me that I don't know what's best for my own son." Marie thinks parents need encouragement to believe in themselves as the experts on their own children. Her experiences may encourage you.

The first in a series of school-related problems occured as Zach finished kindergarten. He was included in the one-third of the class recommended for pre-first grade. Pre-first grade is a transition grade for youngsters not ready for first grade. In some areas these are called *developmental first-grade classes*. Marie questions the whole idea of pre-first grades in the first place. She thinks they wouldn't be needed if first grades were geared for 6-year-olds. She especially questioned such a placement for her child, fearing he would feel labeled as a failure.

Pulling out

Marie decided to defy the placement recommendation and teach Zach at home through a state home-schooling program. She didn't tell Zach about "failing" kindergarten, but that she wanted him home so she could be with him. She persisted in this decision despite criticism that this would damage Zach socially.

Zach's love of learning and questioning mind blossomed during his year of learning at home. Marie said they really had fun. She taught the way she thought education should be. There were lots of field trips to kindle Zach's interest and lots of books on any subject he wanted. Zach wrote to his heart's content, using the family computer. Neighborhood children came over often and Zach got to show them what he was doing. Contrary to dire predictions, Zach's social development improved. He got along better with other kids and dealt better with authority than he had previously. He was feeling very good about himself.

He was ready for second grade the next year and wanted to go back to school. He had an extremely successful year. His second-grade teacher recognized that he was exceptionally bright and accepted his unique need to explore ideas. Mrs. Glenn and Zach liked each other a lot.

Living with the problem

The next year was different. Marie and Mrs. Glenn both looked on in dismay as Zach's self-esteem slipped away. Mrs. X, his third-grade teacher, didn't have a good word to say to or about him. Zach didn't conform to her notion of a good pupil; he had too many ideas of his own. Mrs. X had Zach in the low reading group, which she called her "Bumps on a Log." She didn't seem to understand the devastating effect of her constant criticism and insults. Zach's classmates picked up on the teacher's attitude and began to pick on him, too.

Mrs. Glenn would call him into her room occasionally to try to counteract the negative feedback Zach received from Mrs. X. At home, Marie tried to keep him from becoming totally crushed. She was frustrated because Zach was showing the effects of the problem, but didn't want to talk about it. Zach's temper was short as a result of the pressure. He also burst into tears at the slightest criticism, or even at an offer of help. He just couldn't cope with any more negatives. Worst of all, he was no longer the kind and loving little boy he had been. He began to pick on his little sister, trying to make her feel as bad as he felt.

Marie didn't want to add to the pressure on Zach. She knew he needed to talk, but that he had to feel comfortable first. She finally discovered that a quiet conversation at bedtime was helpful. With the lights low and his mother there to help him feel safe, he could reveal his hurt inside. That was when he would talk about his daily struggle at school.

Marie and Zach's Dad, Ted, were having their own daily struggles at school. They took turns going in to discuss problems with the teacher or principal. After the principal talked to the teacher about balancing criticism with compliments, Mrs. X had a talk with Zach about compliments. She told him, "When I DON'T say anything to you, understand that it means you're doing a good job." Zach's response was, "Well, compliments are real nice to get."

What's education all about?

At parent conference time, Marie and Ted were told that Zach was "learning disabled." The evidence to support this was a sample of Zach's writing. The assignment was to write about a friend. Zach had written a moving account of the special qualities of his best friend. The teacher's response was to mark it all up in red because the handwriting was not neatly on the lines. Zach's apparent inability to make a correct letter "N" was the focus of the parent conference.

"This kind of thing just rips my heart out," Marie tells me. "Here I am trying to raise my child to be a caring person, but all the teacher focuses on is whether his N's are above the line or below it."

It's hard being smart

Zach's parents know that their child isn't learning disabled. They know that he is a gifted child who has trouble conforming to mundane school assignments. They refuse to have him put in a program for learning-disabled students. When the teacher suggests that Zach be tested for learning disabilities, Ted suggests that she look in his file for the test scores already there. At age 7, Zach tested at a 14-year-old level for logic and abstract thinking.

Unfortunately, Zach isn't so confident. He thinks maybe he is retarded and insists on seeing his test scores. Amazingly, it isn't uncommon for gifted children to have a low self-esteem. Being different in any way can cause a child to feel bad. This is especially true when a gifted child has a teacher who doesn't accept individual differences.

Finally, the school year ends. Zach has a summer to recuperate. Marie notices that he is gaining weight and isn't so skinny. It finally dawns on her that stress had been keeping his weight down. During the summer Zach gets to meet his next year's teacher. He really likes Mr. Daniels and is now excited about school. He is looking forward to school so much that he says, "I think I'm going to hate being sick next year." The resilence of children is a wonderful thing.

Disagreeing with the teacher

Jean used a different approach when she was concerned about her daughter's first-grade teacher. She tuned-in to the existence of a problem as a result of picking up her child after school. When she would arrive at the classroom, every day she would see that the teacher had written Moira's name on the chalkboard with an unhappy face drawn beside it. In her gentle way, Jean says, "I wondered why."

Whether it affects her own child or not, Jean doesn't think happy or unhappy faces are appropriate. "I think that the child translates that into being liked or not being liked," Jean explains. She is concerned that it focuses attention on pleasing the teacher instead of on learning.

Moira had already come through one bad year. Her kindergarten experience had left her hating school. Additionally, she had been plagued with headaches since starting school. Jean felt she had to do something. She investigated the classroom situation and discovered that Moira's teacher yelled and snapped her fingers at the children in an effort to control the class. Because Jean was worried about the self-esteem of all the children in the class, she went to the principal.

Having input

The principal told her she had to document the problem before action could be taken. This sounded more confrontive than Jean was comfortable with. But what was she to do?

"First you cry and wring your hands; and then you do something," Jean says wryly. "I flounder around some, but I always feel that one person can make a change." Jean decided that the best way to make a change was by being there. She arranged her work schedule so that she could volunteer to work in the classroom five hours a week. The teacher accepted her offer and Jean became a part of the first-grade experience for her own child and the others in the class.

In order to work effectively with the teacher, Jean had to first work on her feelings about that teacher. She had to rid herself of animosity toward the teacher herself, and reject only the offending behavior. Jean tuned-in to the teacher as a person who was doing the best she could. She realized that Mrs. Y just didn't know much about how to teach first grade or about first graders. She is a good person, however, and didn't mean to be harming children.

Jean had two goals for her volunteer work. One was to introduce more developmentally appropriate kinds of educational activities into the program. The other was to bring love and encouragement to the children. She felt that both were lacking.

Making a difference

Although Jean frequently found herself working with reading groups using approaches she didn't believe in, she felt she could alleviate the damage with her caring attitude. She is convinced that children can endure almost anything as long as they are loved. But she did get to make some changes in the educational program, too. On Friday afternoons Mrs. Y would forego the normal classroom activities and let Jean present a different kind of teaching.

The children looked forward to Fridays. Jean brought them open-ended activities that challenged them to think instead of memorize. They were released from the boring workbooks and allowed out of their seats to choose among the variety of learning experiences Jean presented. They were also encouraged to work together; the week's only interactive learning.

Home support

Jean also made sure that the kinds of learning activities missing at school were readily available at home for Moira. At home, Moira had free access to art supplies, quality children's literature, a cuddly calico cat and playtime with friends. Teaching took such forms as storytime and dictating letters to Grandma.

While she was at school, Jean demonstrated her support of Moira in little ways. She would pat her as she walked by or rub her back for a minute.

Children need open-ended activities to balance a program of closed tasks.

Jean did not talk about Mrs. Y for fear of being disrespectful. But Moira knew her Mom was on her side. At home Jean would hold Moira and rock her to comfort her. They would have conversations focusing on the positive aspects of school.

By the end of the year Moira actually decided she will miss Mrs. Y next year. She was more forgiving than Zach was toward Mrs. X. Zach told his Mom, "If I had the brain of Einstein, it would take me all my life to think of one good thing about that teacher."

Parent commitment

Jean has been actively involved in her children's education since preschool. "I am their mother and I am the most concerned about their best interests. I feel that their education is my responsibility. Sure, I'm flustered and frustrated at times, but I feel sorry for parents who are too intimidated to try." Parents can make a difference. The saga of Ellen's battle for her children's education will show you how much difference.

Children with problems

Ellen has two children with slight physical impairments that make learning difficult for them. Her son Lewis is deaf in one ear. His problem was diagnosed early and he was enrolled in a special Handicapped Preschool Program. The program was a great success for him. He made spectacular progress and was able to start school with no observable evidence of his problem. His speech was normal for his age as was his general language development.

When Ellen discovered her daughter Mary had a problem, she enrolled her in the same school. Ellen was confident of good results, but things were different this time. For one thing, the program had changed. Additionally, Mary's problem is an unusual one: She has no dominant side to her brain. Both sides of her brain are equally strong, whereas most people have one dominant side. This causes her eyes to work independently and affects her eyesight drastically. She couldn't focus within three feet in front of her, only farther away. This made her fall down when she tried to walk and it kept her from being able to feed herself.

Mary needed special glasses to force her eyes to work together and she needed therapy for the same purpose. The Handicapped Preschool Program offered 20 minutes a day of therapy, which was fine with Mary's Mom. But the rest of the 4-1/2-hour day was not okay. It did not offer free play or choices much needed by this 2-1/2-year-old child.

Improper placement

The final straw was when Mary's language abilities began to deteriorate. Ellen discovered that Mary was in the speech-and-language classes for children with handicaps in those areas. This was despite the fact that Mary's language ability was far beyond her years when she started at the school. The classes were causing Mary to regress to the level of the teaching. "She was plugged-in to a program that was not only not relevant, but actually *bad* for her," exclaims Ellen.

She didn't know what she could do about it. She says she had to learn what power she had as a parent. "No one ever told me that I had any rights." She talked to a friend with a Down's Syndrome child and found out that parents can take their special-needs kids out of school if they can provide for their education themselves. Ellen says she found out that "We are in charge of the schools, not the other way around."

A court order

When your child has been identified as handicapped, your parental rights change somewhat. The court gets involved in decisions about his or her education. Ellen and her husband had already trustingly signed the forms for Mary's "Individual Education Plan" better known as the *IEP*. But now they wanted to change their minds. They decided that Mary would be better off if Ellen stayed home and took charge of her eduction. They had to present their case to a judge.

First, Ellen got the support of Mary's therapist. The therapist agreed that Ellen would be able to do the therapy at home, with only weekly visits for supervision. Then Ellen had Mary tested so she could prove that her vocabulary and general language skills had gone down since entering the program. Next, Ellen arranged to provide child care for other children in her home so that Mary would have role models and social interaction. Confronted with this information, the judge ruled in Ellen's favor.

Regular testing during Mary's home schooling showed good progress. In addition, her parents sent her to dance classes, ski lessons, basketball camp—anything to help her with eye-hand coordination and total body coordination. Now that she is kindergarten age, her gross motor skills are up to her age level. Her eye-hand and small motor coordination is only 9 to 12 months behind. Her language skills are two years ahead, however.

Parents and teachers as partners

Mary will attend public school, where she is eligible for a variety of special services. But Ellen will not let her be pulled out of class and made to feel different. She has arranged for Mary's special classes to be after school instead. In addition, Ellen has met with Mary's regular teacher for next year to let her know about Mary's special strengths and weaknesses.

She is still actively involved in Lewis' education, also. She always makes sure teachers know that Lewis is a visual learner, that he needs directions written down instead of told to him. Ellen finds that teachers welcome this kind of information. When a teacher tells her about a problem her child is having, she considers it a request for parental help.

Choosing a reading program

When Lewis was in first grade, Ellen asserted herself about his reading program. She told the teacher, "I love what you are doing with Lewis in Math and Social Studies, and I like how you handle discipline. But I don't like what you are doing in Reading." The teacher agreed that the reading group wasn't working for Lewis.

Ellen suggested that Lewis be allowed to go to the library during reading period. The teacher picked up on the idea and arranged for a group of five children to have reading with the librarian. They went to the library, picked out books, read and discussed them with the librarian. About half-way through the year, they began writing books reports, too. The librarian loved working with children, the kids loved it and everyone was happy. Even the test scores at the end of the year proved that children don't need workbooks to learn to read. All the children in the library reading program had very high scores.

Many child reading problems are a result of teaching that doesn't match how they learn. The kind of fragmented phonics-based instruction that most of us encountered presents learning obstacles. Generally, children learn to read in spite of improper teaching; they manage to make some sense out of print due their real-life experiences with reading. But some children get bogged down in confusion. They begin to doubt themselves and their abilities. Fear gets in the way of learning and they fail.

Sometimes reading problems are a result of physical, emotional or perceptual impediments to learning. Then we need to deal with those impediments. But this doesn't mean further depriving those youngsters of opportunities to learn in meaningful ways. Too often children with observable learning difficulties are placed in programs that provide isolated drill on sub-skills of reading. These approaches do a disservice to a child's literacy development. Intervention programs should help children compensate for the problems that make learning difficult, but should not otherwise treat them differently from other children.

Parent power

Ellen has learned a lot about her power as a parent. She asserts it regularly in picking her children's teachers and in telling them what they need to know about her children. She looks for teachers who are willing to listen to parents. She believes in two-way communication and education as a partnership between parents and teachers. You, too, can make your child's education a team effort between you and the schools.

Signs of School Problems

If your child shows unusual signs of stress such as:
* Headaches
* Crying easily
* General irritability
* Inability to cope with criticism or frustration

If your child begins to doubt himself and so:
* Becomes hesitant to try new things
* Makes negative comments about his abilities
* Starts putting-down others

If your child is unhappy at school and so:
* Doesn't want to go to school
* Feels sick at school time

Parent Response to School Problems

* Provide comfort and support to your child
* Discuss the problem with the teacher
* Observe your child at school
* Determine cause of the problem
* Assert yourself in alleviating the cause
* Remember that parents have the final say

Accomplished, Eager Readers & Writers

Is it worth the effort and energy to nurture your child's growth in literacy? Does it pay off to screen teachers, read endless stories, listen to limitless chatter, try to read senseless scribbles, endure creative-play messes and hope no one sees you playing house?

Where does all this lead? It can lead to a kid like my son David, who doesn't hear what I am telling him because he is engrossed in a book. It can lead to a child who stays up too late at night sometimes because he doesn't want to put his book down. It can lead to parents who have to do a lot of typing because their fourth grader wrote a 135-page book. (Like David, most kids aren't up to

Where does this all lead? . . . possibly to a kid like my son who doesn't hear what I'm telling him because he's so engrossed in a book.

hand copying that much for revisions.) It can lead to kids who spend all their allowance on paperback adventure books. Or, kids who need need rides to the library *right now* because a book on reserve just got in.

Later, it can lead to not having your child home for dinner because of working late on the high-school yearbook. It can even lead to having your child gone for the whole summer as a foreign-exchange student. Eventually, it will lead to having that child leave you and go off to college.

Is it worth it? Looking at my happy, confident son, I say, "No doubt about it."

Bibliography

There is much research available in books and journals about the Whole Language approach to teaching reading and about Developmentally Appropriate Education. Following are some of these books, some of which I used in doing research for this book. I found them fascinating and you may, too.

Cazden, Courtney, ed. *Language in Early Childhood Education*. Washington, D.C.: National Association for the Education of Young Children, 1981.

Cochran-Smith, Marilyn. *The Making of a Reader*. Norwood, N.J.: Ablex, 1984.

de Villiers, Peter A., and Jill G. de Villiers. *Early Language*. Cambridge: Harvard University Press, 1979.

Farr, Marcia, ed. *Children's Early Writing Development*. Norwood, N.J.: Ablex, 1985.

Graves, Donald, and Virginia Stuart. *Write From the Start*. New York: Dutton, 1985.

Goodman, Kenneth. *What's Whole in Whole Language?* Scholastic, Ontario: 1986

Harste, Jerome, Virginia Woodward and Carolyn Burke. *Language Stories and Literacy Lessons*. Portsmouth, N.H.: Heinemann, 1984.

Paley, Vivian. *Wally's Stories*. Cambridge: Harvard University Press, 1981.

Rogers, Cosby, and Janet Sawyers. *Play in the Lives of Children*. Washington, D.C.: National Association for the Education of Young Children, 1988.

Another book I wrote that you might be interested in is: Fields, Marjorie. *Let's Begin Reading Right*. Columbus: Merrill, 1987. This book for teachers is about beginning literacy. You may find it interesting.

These worthwhile journals can be found in most libraries:
> *Language Arts*
> *Reading Teacher*
> *Young Children*

In addition to information found in the above books and journals, the periodical *Parent's Magazine* frequently has excellent articles.

Index

A

active 39
active learning 225
activities 86, 140, 167
activities, closed 259
activities, open-ended 259
alphabet 146, 156
authority, deal with 252

B

baby talk 29, 74
basics 140
being smart 255
book reports, writing 265
books 69, 103, 106-107, 136-137, 187, 218, 221, 223, 269

C

child-care center 177
classroom volunteer 257
coloring books 173
comfort 251
compliments 254

computer 172, 204, 209, 241, 246
computer games 225
computer, write with 252
context 78, 122
    clues 75
contextual 65
contextualized print 144, 234
controlled vocabulary 243
conversation 64, 66-67, 77, 119, 123-124
court order 262
criticism 32
    effect of 253

D

development 70
dictates 189
dictation 147, 149, 235
discover 10
Down's Syndrome 262
dramatic play 165, 230
drawing 102, 160, 173
drill 70

E

editing 209, 245
education
    early-childhood 241,
    250
    goals of 254
elaboration 81
emotional development
    165
errors 205, 216
experience 134, 180
experience of 91
experiences 36, 39, 43,
    122, 131, 139-140,
    225, 227
exploration 51

F

family home child-care
    77
final say, parents have
    251
first-grade 242, 244
flash cards 58, 70

G

gifted children 255
glasses, special 261
grammar 30, 79-80, 116,
    124
group size 177

H

handicapped preschool
    program 260-261
handicaps, speech-and-
    language classes for
    261
home schooling 263
home support 258
home therapy 263
home-schooling
    program 252

I

Individual Education
    Plan (IEP) 263
insults, effect of 253
intellectual
development 50, 88, 165
instruction, directed 58,
    217
interactive learning 258
invented spelling 16, 30,
    199, 206

J

judge 263

K

kindergarten 242, 244

L

language 23, 26, 61, 63,

65, 67, 73, 77, 82, 91, 103, 115, 117, 119, 124, 199, 233
    acquisition 74, 80
learning, disabled 255
learning, discovery 15
learning disabilities, testing for 255
letter-like forms 159
letter-like stage 13
literacy development 265
loved children 258
low self-esteem 251, 255

M
maturation 64, 80, 116, 130, 216
maturity 216
misspellings 242
mistake 37
model of 81
motherese 61
multi-age grouping 187

N
names 145, 197, 235
negative feedback 253

O
overgeneralization 31

P
parent commitment 260
parent power 265
parents who work 56
partners, teachers and parents 264
penmanship 206, 246
phonics 9, 17, 20, 206, 220, 240
placement, improper 261
play 161, 163, 169, 183, 230, 244, 248
play dough 86
play materials 172
play times 170
practice 53, 100, 119
practicing 62
preschool 177
print-rich environment 3
problems, children with 260
pronunciation 81
punctuation 209, 211, 245

Q
questions 81, 125, 130, 154

R
reading period 264

reading program,
      choosing 264
role models 263

S
school asignments,
      mundane 255
school problems, parent
      response to 266
school problems, signs
      of 266
school, problems at 251
schools, intimidated by
      251
scribble stage 11
scribbles 97, 154, 196
self-correction 32
self-esteem 88, 257
senses 53
sentences 79, 124
sight-word vocabulary 9
skills 139, 150
social development 252
social interaction 263
sound substitutions 79
speech 23-24, 62, 74, 118
spelling 19, 151, 195-
      196, 206, 211, 245,
      248
stories 133, 220
story interpretation 130
storytime 104, 107, 127,
      131

stuttering 116
support 251
symbolic representation
      41, 43, 160-161, 163,
      173

T
talk 61, 78, 123
teachers 183
      disagreeing with 256
      find 251
      work with 257
television 130, 219, 225
The Language
      Experience Approach
      to Reading 9
therapist 263
therapy, home 263
training of preschool
      teachers 178
trouble-shooting 251-266

V
vocabulary 73-74, 77,
      103, 115, 124, 214,
      231

W
Whole Language
      philosophy x, 3, 250
workbooks 206, 237, 240
workbooks, boring 258

worksheets 158, 179
write 44-45
writing 7, 11-12, 15-16,
    19, 24, 97-98, 100,
    102, 149, 151, 154,
    156, 159, 173, 188,
    195, 199-200, 206,
    208, 211, 213, 235,
    237, 242, 248
workbook, materials 97
writing center 158, 187
writing, teaching about
    154